*SEEKING
THE ABSOLUTE LOVE*

SEEKING
THE ABSOLUTE LOVE

THE FOUNDERS OF
CHRISTIAN MONASTICISM

Mayeul de Dreuille OSB

Gracewing.

A Herder & Herder Book
The Crossroad Publishing Company
New York

First published in 1999
jointly by

Gracewing
2 Southern Ave,
Leominster
Herefordshire
HR6 0QF

The Crossroad Publishing Company
370 Lexington Avenue
New York
NY 10017
USA

UK ISBN 0 85244 468 0

US ISBN 0 8245 1830 6
Library of Congress Catalog Number 99-74245

cum permissu Superiorum

Typesetting by
Action Publishing Technology Ltd, Gloucester, GL1 1SP

Printed in England by
Redwood Books Ltd,
Trowbridge, Wiltshire, BA14 8RN

Contents

INTRODUCTION

Legend recounts that St Benedict wrote his Rule at the dictation of an angel. Recent studies, however, show that his genius lay in choosing, with consummate skill, the essential traits of the monastic tradition and in integrating them into the Roman life of his time.

Our age poses for all Christian Religious a similar problem, namely, how to adapt oneself to a changing civilization. Moreover, the Church asks people, all over the world, to create a religious life in harmony with their own culture. Experience shows that one of the great difficulties in integrating the Christian tradition into a new culture is the lack of points of comparison allowing us to distinguish essential values from those that vary with age. To achieve this adaptation, St Benedict made a skilful selection from the treasures of experience gathered by the ancients. At the end of his Rule, he invites us to imitate him, and my work is an attempt to answer his invitation.

A few years ago, when I was in India, I published three books: one on the Fathers, another on St Benedict and the third on the history of monasticism. These are now out of print, but the interest they aroused has led me to present the material in a slightly different way. One volume gives the history of monasticism, before and after Christ, in the Asian religions and in Christendom. The other (this present work) gives the teaching of the founders of Christian monasticism, up to Saint Bernard.

The title of this book *Seeking the Absolute Love* means that I have tried to let each author explain the way he found to move towards the God of Jesus Christ, the God of Love.

As the reader thus makes a living contact with the founders of the 'Monastic Order', he may, perhaps, be able to capture their spirit and so contribute to the contemporary development of an authentic religious life in harmony with the past and integrated into the culture of each country.

I have now to express my gratitude, not only to the persons who helped me to publish the first version of this work but also to those who assisted me in bringing it up to date. First of all, I thank the Patriarchs of the Orthodox Churches and the Ecumenical Secretariat of Lausanne, for the information about monastic life in their Churches. My thanks go also to Fr C. Dumont O.C.S.O. for 'Saint Bernard' and to Fr A. de Vogüé O.S.B., who agreed to revise the whole text and give me the results of the latest historical research on the beginnings of monasticism in the West.

I hope that this study of the roots common to all Christian monasticism will also contribute to a mutual understanding between the Churches, in the love of Christ.

CHAPTER I

Clement of Alexandria

ALEXANDRIA

Alexandria was a flourishing commercial city and was the centre of a brilliant intellectual culture. Influences coming from the Far East, from India, from Greece and Rome met here to form a new kind of civilization. For the Jews, too, it provided a favourable terrain for attempting to establish a link between the teaching of the Old Testament and Greek speculation. The translation of the Septuagint and several of the Wisdom books were the first fruits of this Jewish-Hellenic culture, which afterwards developed into a whole literature of which Philo was the most outstanding writer.

When Christianity reached this city at the end of the first century, it had to come to grips with these diverse influences. To adapt herself to the life around her, the Church abandoned the rigidity of Jewish observance, to accept what was best in Hellenistic humanism. On the cultural level she reaped the heritage of Greek rhetoric and philosophy and used it to deepen her understanding of the Christian revelation. Here we have the elements that form the outstanding features of the School of Alexandria: interest in metaphysics, researches into faith, a tendency to use the philosophy of Plato and the allegorical interpretation of Scripture.

It was in Egypt that the first Christian monastic institution was formed. The Alexandrine Fathers, Clement, his teacher Pantaenus and later, Origen, developed the ideas on which monastic life was founded and developed. It is important to study their thought on the points that concern us.

The Life and Works of Clement of Alexandria

Clement was the disciple and successor of Pantaenus. The latter was probably a Judeo-Christian, who, after a missionary journey to India, undertook the task of combining Christian doctrine with the teachings of Greek philosophy. He died at Alexandria shortly before the year A.D. 200.

Clement was born of pagan parents either at Athens or Alexandria. He received a brilliant education, and, after his conversion to Christianity, travelled in Italy, Syria and Palestine, in search of instruction from the most notable Christian teachers, until, attracted by the reputation of Pantaenus, he finally settled at Alexandria to follow his lectures. He remained as assistant and then as successor to his master, and became a presbyter of the church. The persecution of Septimus Severus forced him to flee to Cappadocia and Palestine. He died about A.D. 215.

His principal writings are: the *Protrepticus* or 'An exhortation' to the Greeks; the *Paedagogus* or 'The Tutor' in which he teaches the converted pagan how to organize his whole life in a Christian manner; and, finally, the *Stromata* or 'Miscellanies' which deal with a variety of subjects.

Clement's teaching holds a special interest for us because it shows Christianity facing a different culture for the first time and also because his description of the perfect Christian was later to influence monasticism.

Doctrine

Encounter of Christianity with non-Christian cultures

In the person of this highly educated Greek, the faith, received from the Judeo-Christian community, confronted Hellenistic culture at its best. It was Clement's aim to retain all true values reaped from his education and integrate them into the faith. To give his synthesis a rational basis, he propounded an interesting theory that in the beginning God sent angels to communicate to each race a specific wisdom which in time had decayed. (*Strom. I. VI. VII; Strom. VI. 17–161. 2. 3*). A particular interest was invested in that given to the Hebrews, but others had their value, and Clement compares their wise men to the prophets of Israel.

The unique Word, he maintained, gave to each nation the form of wisdom suited to it: a wisdom, one in principle but multiform in presentation. The Word manifested itself personally in Christ, but the same pattern remains; Christ's revelation assumes forms appropriate to the various cultures. If Christianity is to penetrate into the Greek world, it must abandon its Semitic garb and speak the language of Plato, though without falling into syncretism. While remaining faithful to the Gospel, Christians should express it in a manner similar to that followed by the Heroes whom the Greeks take as models for their social life.[1] Christianity is the true 'philosophy', the true wisdom; it fulfils the ideal proposed by the Greek Sages, who had themselves borrowed it from the 'Barbarians'.

> For philosophy, so necessary to the right conduct of life, had flourished in ancient times among the wise men of foreign nations, in forms suited to the different races. Among them, the chief were the prophets of Egypt, the Chaldeans of Assyria, the Druids of Gaul and the Celtic philosophers, the Magi of Persia and the Gymnosophists of India. There were also schools of philosophy among the Sarmans[2] and Brahmins, and in India those who followed the precepts of Buddha. (*Strom. I. 15, 71, 3–6*)

Those wise men no doubt lacked the high inspiration of the Hebrew prophets, but God had bestowed on them 'a certain gleam of truth', as though 'by reflection or seen through a glass,' (*Strom. I. 19–24, 7*) or given them help of some kind. (*Ped. II. 28*)

> Divine power, inspiring the mind, endows it with vigour and keenness of perception, filling it with eagerness and courage in thought or in action. The clearest manifestation of this is expressed in the Covenants or in the laws of the Hellenes, but it is found also in the teachings of philosophy. (*Strom. VI. 17, 161, 2, 3*).[3]

It is then useful to study philosophy, rejecting only perversions that have crept into it. Here Clement is at one with Justin who had said of the pagans: 'All that is good in their teaching belongs to us Christians also.' (*Apol. 13*)

Philo had already worked along the same lines. In his Biblical exposition he had employed the allegorical method favoured by the Greeks in their exegesis of Homer and Hesiod, and had used it for the same reason – to interpret unedifying stories and antiquated laws for his own generation. Clement went a step further. He applied this and other scholarly techniques of Greek philosophers to Christianity. To arrive at a closer understanding of the texts, he employed etymology, grammar and dialectical reasoning, and laid the foundation of the theological method by linking the data of Scripture with the essential principles of revealed truth, thus passing, according to his own account, from simple faith to knowledge or *gnosis*.

The perfect Christian, the Gnostic

Clement wished to present to cultured people of his time, the pattern of a thoroughly Christian man, that was at the same time consistent with the Hellenistic ideal. The goal to be achieved was contemplation of and unceasing union with the Godhead.

Stromata VII enumerates several stages in the progress towards contemplation: 'movement from heathenism to faith, from faith to knowledge, from knowledge to love and from love to the inheritance.' (*Strom. VII. 10*)

By 'faith' or *pistis* Clement understands the starting point of conversion and a comprehensive knowledge of essentials, which have to be perfected by knowledge or *gnosis*.

Gnosis or knowledge discerns and holds fast to the true God. This implies 'long preparation and serious training', which includes the development of some of the main aspects of Christian life:

A Christian should first of all fulfil the duties that fall on every man, 'regarding nothing as evil except ignorance and actions contrary to right reason', (*Strom. VI. 4*) as well as obedience to God's commands and the practice of all in imitation of the Lord. (*Strom. VII. 3, 12*)

Schooling in God's law is also necessary before a man can practise it and even 'go intelligently beyond the righteousness of the Law.' Knowledge of Scripture is useful in refuting heresy, (*Strom. VII. 16*) but secular learning, as we have already said, can contribute to the understanding of Scripture. (*Strom. I, 1, 5, 6, 7, 11; and Strom. VIII*)

Detachment is the fruit of knowing the only good – and of concentration upon it alone. 'Knowledge is purifying' (*Strom. VII. 10*); it begins with repentance (*Strom. VII. 14*), separates from the passions and from what is purely pleasurable, and leads to a life of virtue. (*Strom. VII. 12*)

Control over the passions and even the desire for good culminates in *apatheia*, that is in moderation and perfect calmness. It is marked by steadfast attachment to the essential good and an assimilation to Him 'who by nature possesses impassibility – *apatheia*'. This idea of *apatheia* as a state of deep tranquillity and a consequence of perfect self-mastery, would be taken up later by several monastic writers.

Virginity is an expression of detachment, but it is holy only when it springs from love of God. (*Strom. III. 6*) Clement does not emphasize it however, for he is preoccupied with defending Christian marriage against various forms of Encratism.[4] (*Strom. III*) He even goes so far as to say that the difficulties inherent in married life are such that were a married man to reach perfection, 'he would surpass all other men'.

Beyond faith and knowledge there is a third stage leading to contemplation that is *agape* or love. 'Knowledge terminates in love; love gives the loving to the lover, that which knows to that which is known.' (*Strom. VII. 10*) Perfection does not lie in intellectual contemplation, but in love and especially in love of Christ, 'through whom we have converse with God.' (*Strom. VII. 3*)

Praise and self-oblation are the highest expression of love. 'We glorify Him who gave himself in sacrifice for us, and we, in turn, sacrifice ourselves.' (*Strom. VII. 3*) Love begins with benevolence towards one's neighbour; in its supreme form it is also a redemptive activity. The essential value of martyrdom is not in its heroism but in that 'it shows the perfection of charity.'

> The Apostles, imitating their Lord, in true and perfect knowledge, gave their lives for the churches they had founded. So, the man versed in knowledge, walking in the steps of the Apostles, must be without sin. His love for his neighbour will be the fruit of his love for the Lord and then, faced with a crisis, he will bear the ordeal without faltering and drink the chalice for the sake of the Church. (*Strom. IV*)

Clement gives the name of 'martyr' to the gnostic who has reached ordinary union with God, (*Strom. IV. 14–96*) for he is a witness to the love of God and to the presence of the Spirit who accomplishes in man what is beyond human power to achieve.[5]

All this process of purification is enveloped in prayer and culminates in 'an uninterrupted dialogue and fellowship with God.' (*Strom. VII. 3*) Clement repeatedly asserts that prayer must accompany all the actions of the day:

> Not only on rising, in the morning and at noon, but also when walking about, when dressing and undressing. (*Strom. VII. 2*)
> Convinced that God surrounds us on all sides, we praise Him as we cultivate our fields, and we sing hymns as we sail the sea. (*Strom. VII. 7*)

For certain men, advanced in *gnosis*, Clement seems to envisage a life given up completely to prayer:

> Their whole life is a holy festival ... prayers, praise and reading from the Scriptures before meals, psalms and hymns during the meal and before retiring to rest, and more prayers during the night. Thus they unite themselves to the choir of heaven, and pass from unbroken recollection to eternal contemplation. (*Strom. VII. 7*)

This continual prayer has greater value than that which is said at fixed times:

The soul, purified by knowledge, is led by prayer and love 'through the various stages of mystical progress, until the pure heart reaches that crowning place of rest, the vision of God, face to face' ... There 'the only-begotten Son stamps the seal of contemplation on him, according to His own image.' (*Strom. VIII. 3*)

Clement does not conceal the fact that he is speaking purely on the theoretical level, where 'it is possible that such a man may reach a stage of equality with the angels'. But the very hope of seeing God in this way encourages the man who 'by ceaseless endeavour, presses on to reach the Lord's own mansion, alert, steadfast, persevering and wholly and in every part unchangeable.' (*Strom. VII. 10*)

This idea of a state of perfect contemplation accorded to men here on earth, is evidently erroneous, and Clement can be censured also for asserting that the prayers of the gnostic are always heard, while those of the less worthy are rarely granted.

On the other hand, his great devotion to Christ is clear: it is with Christ that the gnostic holds 'uninterrupted converse'. Christ is the model: He is the way to God. Through imitating Him the soul is transformed into His image and shares His redemptive activity.

The task of the perfect gnostic is to converse with God through His great High-Priest and, as far as he is able, to become like Him by offering God every form of service. This service is concerned with the salvation of men, for the Gnostic shares in God's care and kindness towards us, and it includes the adoration (given to God), the teaching (imparted to men), and his works of charity.

Finally a special chapter (*Strom. VII. 9*) is devoted to the gnostic who has undertaken to teach others. The teacher must 'excel in virtue' and has a particular dignity because he represents God and leads men to him:

The true greatness of the Word is conveyed to men, who are God's living images, by a trustworthy teacher, and men impute the kindness the teacher shows them to the Lord Himself; for, like the Lord, the gnostic, although a mere man, teaches, fashions, transforms, and renews the catechumen for his salvation. (*Strom. VII. 9*)

Clement's work, continuing that of the apologists, of the second century, freed Christians from the ghetto. They now entered fully into the civilization of their time and used its riches to benefit their faith. His studies in theology and mysticism opened the way for the great men of the third century, while the concept of a life consecrated entirely to God was soon to blossom into Christian monasticism.

Notes

1   J. Daniélou, *Nouv. Histoire de l'Eglise* p. 164; see also: *Message Evangélique et Culture Hellénistique au 2e et 3e Siècles*, pp. 41–72.
2   'Sarmans': Ascetics, in sanscrit 'sramanas'.
3   cf. J. Daniélou, *Message ...* (op. cit.) p. 52ss.
4   Clement presents the Christian as the true gnostic in opposition to the non-Christian or heretic gnostic currents of thought prevailing in his time. Gnosticism is based on two dualisms. The first recognizes the existence of a good divinity dwelling in light, and in opposition to it there is a *demiurge*, the creator of the world of ignorance, matter and darkness. The second dualism is found in man between the spark of divine light and the material body in which it is imprisoned by the demiurge.
     In the moral sphere *gnosis* considers the world and matter as intrinsically evil. They are overcome by extreme asceticism or a higher knowledge, *gnosis,* received by revelation of a divine Messenger, which transforms the soul and enables her to distinguish between good and evil. Thus raised above the laws of the ordinary world, she becomes able to escape into the kingdom of light.
     The doctrine of Clement is a remarkable attempt to sift all the truths contained in these theories and to lead them to their crowning in the love of Christ and fraternal charity. On the other hand he is opposing the exaggerated asceticism of heretics like Encratists, based on these dualist theories.
     Dualism with the consequent despising of matter and of the body will remain a permanent temptation for Christian monachism, but it will provoke also the healthy reaction of most of the great monastic Fathers.
5   cf. J. Daniélou, *The First Six Hundred Years*, p. 126.

CHAPTER II

Origen

His life and works

Origen was born in A.D. 185 in Alexandria,[1] the eldest son of a large family. After the martyrdom of his father, Leonidas, during the persecution of Septimus Severus in A.D. 200, the young man, filled with a passionate desire to die a martyr himself, consecrated his life to God. His father had given him a sound education based on the study of both sacred Scripture and secular subjects. Under the persecution, the state confiscated his patrimony and he was obliged to support his mother and brothers and sisters by becoming a teacher himself.

Already famous for his zeal in supporting the martyrs and for his brilliant teaching, Origen was appointed head of the catechetical school, despite his youth, in place of his master, Clement, who had been forced to flee. He held this post from A.D. 203 to 230, but soon, following the example of Clement, he entrusted the beginners to an assistant and devoted himself to lecturing on Philosophy and Scripture to advanced students. While occupying this position, he attended the lectures of Ammonius Saccas, a notable Neo-Platonist, who was later to become the master of Plotinus, twenty years Origen's junior.

About 230, difficulties arose with the Bishop of Alexandria and Origen left for Caesaria in Palestine, where he established a school over which he presided for twenty years. During the Decian persecution, he was subjected to prolonged tortures which led to his death shortly afterwards at Tyre in A.D. 253.

His writings are numerous; those that have come down to us can be grouped into several categories. In the first place come works of textual criticism, in which he collates various versions of the Bible in parallel columns. Some books, the *Hexapla*, are in six versions; others, the *Tetrapla*, are in four; the Psalms or *Henneapla* are in nine.

His exegetical works are commentaries (*scholia*) and homilies on selected passages of the Bible. He also wrote commentaries on St Matthew, St John, the Epistle to the Romans and the Song of Songs. In studying the texts, he deals briefly with the literal sense, attaching more importance to the mystical meaning, revealed through allegory.

He wrote also a treatise on apologetics, *Against Celsus*, a pagan philosopher, a work admired by his contemporary scholars. To these expositions of Scripture he added dogmatic writings – *De principiis* or *First Principles*, the earliest synthesis of Ecclesiastical doctrine, and *The Stromata*, a miscellany, a comparison of Christian doctrine, with pagan philosophy. Finally we have his ascetical works – *On Prayer*, an important treatise on the spiritual life, and *Exhortation to Martyrdom*, an expression of his ardent love for Christ.

His monastic doctrine

Origen frequently praised withdrawal from the world or spiritual *anachoresis*.[2] He speaks of separation from the life, thoughts and desires of the world in order to concentrate entirely on the service of God. It was in this light that he interpreted the Exodus from Egypt, the Sabbath rest, and the life of John the Baptist in the desert; these symbolize the surrender of all that hinders the ideal of living with God in an ardent desire for uninterrupted attention to the things of heaven.

He lived a kind of common life with his closest disciples, with reading of Scripture followed by meditation in the morning and sacred reading again during meals.[3]

Within this group and for all his students, he became the Spiritual Father, devoting himself to their religious training. He taught them what he called the 'philosophic life'[4] or the 'life of wisdom.' This consisted of self-knowledge and scrutiny of one's actions in order to seek only the good of the soul. This good lies above all in the love of the Logos, the divine Word, who by His wonderful beauty attracts the soul and shares with it His own divine life and truth. It is necessary to be acquainted with the different schools of philosophy, for they help to reveal the truth contained in Scripture,[5] but the master's chief role is to lead his disciples to the only true teacher, the Divine Master who leads the soul progressively towards union with God.[6]

The scheme of spiritual ascent first outlined by Clement was developed by Origen in a systematic exposition of mystical experience based on the spiritual sense of the Bible, in which he enumerates its main stages.[7] Owing to its Biblical inspiration, Origen's work has exerted a lasting influence on later writers such as Gregory of Nyssa, Evagrius, Cassian, Pseudo-Dionysius, Augustine, Bernard and Bonaventure.

The first stage in the ascent to God is conversion.[8] This is brought about when man realizes that whereas he was created in the image of God, that image has been defaced by sin, and to recover its true nature it must be restored by conformity to the Logos. (The distinction between the transcendant essence of the Trinity and the divinization of the soul by God's grace was not formulated until the fourth century. In Origen, the soul's kinship with the divine is considered as a natural property.) At this stage, faith is of primary importance.

The second stage is that of union with God. This is symbolized by the Jewish Exodus, as Origen explains in his homilies on Exodus and Numbers.[9] The halting-places in the desert represent the various stages of the soul's progress towards God, and correspond to the purgative and illuminative ways.

The first period is marked by a struggle against sin and the passions, which leads to the acquisition of *apatheia* or spiritual freedom, the fruit of self-mastery and detachment that makes recollection possible.

The second period sees the transformation of the soul by progressive illumination and spiritual trials. It is characterized by the formation in the soul of a true estimate of all things,[10] and by the realization of the nothingness of all that is temporal. Here the soul is made to understand that the spiritual world is the sole reality.

Origen lays stress on the fact that the spiritual life is a matter of continual progress, symbolized by the image of the tabernacle that was constantly moved from one resting place in the desert to another.[11] Nevertheless the nearer a man approaches God's wisdom, the more difficult he finds it to express this in words.

But all these graces are not given as an aid to self-centred contemplation. Origen considers the struggle against sin as part of the cosmic battle between good and evil, in which, tempted by demons and helped by angels, the ascetic and the martyr fight on behalf of the Church and for all men.[12] Grace, strength and illumination are given to enable the soul to fight more successfully against the various aspects of evil; sin, heresy and pagan philosophies.[13]

The climax of this second stage is *ecstasis*, which Origen interprets as awe before the 'things great and wonderful'[14] contemplated in prayer. He distrusts physical ecstasy because of the excesses committed by the Montanists.[15]

The third stage is that of perfect union in love. Origen develops this theme in his commentary on the Song. 'The soul perfected in morals and trained in discernment, is able to rise to the contemplation of the divinity by spiritual love',[16] and, having beheld the beauty of God, loves His splendour and receives from Him the arrow that wounds with love.[17] To experience this union demands a special illumination from the Word of God himself, for human resources are unequal to the task. To describe it, Origen employs the image of spiritual senses,[18] special gifts of God enabling the soul to taste and see Him in a manner beyond physical perception.

A general remark must be made about Origen's exposition of the spiritual life. Like Clement, he uses Platonic concepts and vocabulary. This explains one of the limitations of his spiritual theology: He does not take into account the part played by darkness in the life of the soul, but focuses his attention solely on its illumination by the Word. It is significant that he makes the Promised Land the end of the journey, without any mention of Mount Sinai where God was met in a dark cloud, although this event held an important place in Philo and Clement. It was reserved for Gregory of Nyssa to explore this region of the mystical experience. The main merit of Origen's spiritual theology is rather to have opened new perspectives by treating for the first time themes which later became part of the monastic tradition.

Among these themes one of the most important is Virginity.[19] Origen is the first to speak of Mary's perpetual virginity. Marriage is a symbol of the union between Christ and the Church. Virginity affects this union and sets us free in order to serve God. It is a restoration of the state of Paradise on earth, of the life of the prophets. Like martyrdom it is a gift from God and must be preserved by penance and control of the emotions. Virginity of heart is more important than bodily virginity; the latter should be chosen for spiritual purposes alone. Through virginity Christ becomes the bridegroom of the soul. This idea is applied by St Paul to the Church as a whole; Origen applies it to the individual Christian. Spiritual ascent, of which we have already spoken, is also expressed by the image of birth and growth of the Logos, whose interior mission in every soul accomplishes its individual redemption.[20]

Transfiguration is the summit of the spiritual ascent and only those who by unremitting effort undertake the climb are enabled to perceive Christ's transforming light.[21]

The five spiritual senses[22] are Origen's interpretation of Biblical anthropomorphic terms, that is, the attribution to God of human qualities. Sight represents illumination by grace; touch, the experience of God's action in the soul etc. This is the first expression of the doctrine of the gifts of the Holy Spirit, which put the soul into direct contact with the Divine.

Divine light is a gift that enables the soul to see and, at the same time, illumines the object seen by faith. The light originates in the Father, is transmitted to the two other divine Persons, and is reflected by the Church and the saints as sunlight is by the moon and stars.[23]

The Logos transmits the light and it becomes food.[24]

14   *Seeking the Absolute Love*

Sustained by His eternal generation from the Father, He gives and adapts His divinity to souls,[25] feeding them with knowledge of His mysteries.[26] He is comparable also to wine,[27] for He fills the soul with ardour and knowledge of Himself beyond human capacity[28] and supports it in its search for God both in consolation and desolation. Origen carefully distinguishes this charismatic enthusiasm from the states of trance provoked by pagan cults and condemns these states as unnatural.

Scripture is for Origen an inexhaustible source. He possessed a true gift of spiritual understanding, perceiving that in the Bible God often makes use of image and symbol to help man to discover His true nature. To penetrate into the meaning of these mysteries calls for purification of the heart and for constant reading and meditation on the Scriptures. Knowledge of God is inseparable from love of Him and union with Him.

Origen was one of the greatest thinkers of mankind. His genius opened an immense field for the theology of the following centuries. He contributed to great improvements in the expression of the doctrines of the Holy Trinity and the Redemption. His perception of God's word in Scripture, his study of the soul's stages in her ascension towards God and his observation of her reactions under the influence of grace laid the foundations of modern mystical theology. If the wide stream of ideas he set going carried with it some errors, it should be pointed out that he always wanted to be an orthodox Christian, that his burning love for Christ attracted to God a great number of eminent men, and finally that he sealed his faith with his blood. It is mostly under his influence that Christian monachism started its development in Egypt.

Notes

1 On Origen's life see R. Cadiou, *La Jeunesse d'Origéne, Histoire de l'Ecole d'Alexandrie au IIIe Siécle*; J. Daniélou, *Origen*, Book I and *The First Six Hundred Years*. One of the main sources of information on Origen is Eusebius of Caesarea in his *Historia Ecclesiastica*, specially book VI.
2 cf. H. Crouzel: Origéne précurseur du monachisme, in *Théologie de*

la Vie Monastique ch I. Part of our quotations of Origen's works are borrowed from this article.

3 St. Jerome in his *Letter XLIII to Marcella* quotes a letter written to Origen by his disciple and benefactor Ambrose, where it is said that during the day and part of the night 'reading and meditation followed each other in turn' cf. H. Crouzel op. cit. p. 19; see also Origen's *De Oratione* XII, 2; *Contra Celsum* VII, 17–18.

4 Eusebius *Hist. Eccles.* III, 8–12.

5 On non-Christian philosophies useful for the knowledge of the divine and of the Bible see *Hom. in Lev.* V, 8; *Hom. in Genesis* XI, 2.

6 God the only true teacher, see *Com. in I Co.* and *Scholia in Apocalyp.* IX. Origen gives also this meaning to the Visitation: Mary brings Jesus to John, moulding his 'Voice' at the image of the Word. She imparts also to him the Holy Spirit, whom he will communicate to his father and mother, cf. *Com. in Jo.* VI, 49.

7 On Origen's mysticism see Daniélou: *Origen*, book IV. L. Bouyer: *La Spiritualité du N.T. et des Pères*, ch. XII. Most of our quotations on this question come from these two books. See also O. Rousscau: Introduction, in *Homélies sur le Cantique* (Sources Chrétiennes 37).

8 *Hom. in Gen.* I, 13–15.

9 See specially 27th *Hom. in Num.*

10 Origen speaks at length of discernment of spirits in the *De Principiis*.

11 For example in *Hom. in Num.* XVII. 4, 5.

12 See for example *Hom. in Jesus Nave* XIV & XV.

13 *Hom. in Lev.* X, 2; *Hom. in Gen.* XI, 2.

14 *Hom. in Num.* XXVII, 12.

15 Montanism, an apocalyptic heresy proclaiming exaggerated austerity and mysticism.

16 *Com. in Cant.* 78. This text makes an important step in the history of Christian mysticism by distinguishing the purgative, illuminative and unitive ways.

17 *Com. in Cant.* I.

18 *Com. in Cant.* I.

19 cf. H. Crouzel, op. cit. p. 28–31.

20 G. Aeby in *Les Mission divines de Justin à Origène*, collects the texts of Origen where the spiritual ascension is seen as the birth and growth of the Logos in the soul.

21 This theme is developed mostly in Origen's last works.

22 cf. *De Principiis*, I, 7, 9; *Com. in Cant.* 104–105. The development of this theme shows that Origen's spirituality is not mere speculation but rather some knowledge of the divine, coming from a mystical experience, having some similarity with that of St Gregory of Nyssa, St Augustine, St Bernard and St Theresa of Avila who speaks of the 'divine touch'.

23 *Com. in Jo.* I.

24 *Com. in Jo.* XXXII, 24.

25 'Each one is illuminated according to the measure of light he can receive', *Hom. in Gen.* I, 8; cf. also *Cont. Cels.* II, 63.

26 *Hom. in Lev.* VII, 5; VI, 387; *Hom. in Ex.* XIII, 3; *Hom. in Gen.* XI, 3.
27 *Hom. in Num.* XVI, 9; VII, 152; XVII, 9.
28 Spiritual inebriation: *Com. Serm. Mt.* 85. *Com. in Jo.* I, 30.

CHAPTER III

St Antony

Antony and Athanasius

Following the example of the first community of Jerusalem, many Christians both men and women, dedicated their lives to God in prayer, poverty and celibacy. At the end of the persecutions the peace enjoyed by the Church coupled with a reaction against the worldliness that invaded her owing to State protection, multiplied the numbers of these ascetics. They lived apart, either alone or in small groups and gradually Christian monasticism as a normal institution of the Church developed among them. This assumed various forms according to the religious culture of each place.

The life of Antony, an Egyptian solitary, is the first biography of a monk whish has come down to us. Its author, St Athanasius, bishop of Alexandria, was a leading figure of the Church, famous for the part he played in the Council of Nicaea, and his resistance to the powerful heresy of Arianism. This life of Antony,[1] translated early into Latin and widely circulated, contributed powerfully to the growth of monasticism. It defined and propagated, both in the East and in the West, the monastic ideal which 'Antony himself had learned from the Scriptures'.[2] The facts reported of Antony's life are undeniably true: Athanasius was his personal friend and wrote the life within a few years, if not in the actual year of Antony's death. From this account of his life, we can see that successive changes of place divided it into several periods, corresponding to the stages of Antony's spiritual ascent.

LIFE OF ST ANTONY BY ST ATHANASIUS

Vocation

Antony was an Egyptian belonging to a well-to-do
Christian family. When he was about twenty years old, his
parents died, leaving to him the care of the property and of
his young sister:

> Less than six months after his parents' death, as he
> walked to church, he was meditating on the way the
> apostles left everything to follow the Saviour, and on the
> passage in *Acts* which tells how the people sold what they
> had and laid it at the feet of the apostles for distribution
> to the poor. He thought of the treasure laid up in heaven
> for men such as these. He entered the church just as the
> Gospel was being read aloud, and heard the words Our
> Lord addressed to the rich man: 'If thou wilt be perfect,
> go, sell all thou hast, and give it to the poor, and come,
> follow me and thou shalt have treasure in heaven.' As
> though God had given him the mind of the saints, and as
> though the reading had been directed especially to him,
> Antony immediately left the church and gave to the
> townspeople the property he had from his forbears.[3]

Antony leaves the world

Having consigned his sister to the care of 'known and
trusted virgins', Antony retired to a hut near his own house
and put himself under the direction of one of the ascetics
living in the next village. There he devoted his time to
constant prayer, penance and manual work. He gave to the
poor what he did not use for his own sustenance, visited the
other ascetics of the neighbourhood, and 'set out to learn
for his own profit how each excelled him in zeal and morti-
fied life. He admired the graciousness of one, the patience
or charity of another ... in all alike he observed both devotion to Christ and mutual love.'[4]

The tomb

Later he took up his abode far away from the village, in a tomb or little mausoleum, a one-roomed house for the dead. There he lived immured for about fifteen years, a friend of his supplying him at regular intervals with bread, and possibly, too, with the 'bread from heaven'. The symbolism of the tomb should not be ignored, for in baptism, the Christian dies to his former self in order to rise with Christ to a new life. It turned out to be a time of severe trial for Antony. He was assailed by every kind of temptation, impurity, fear, discouragement. The demon even went so far as to beat him to the point of death. His friend found him unconscious and carried him to the church, believing him to be dead, but he awoke during the night and insisted on returning to the tomb.[5]

What is chiefly striking about Antony's struggles is his attachment to Christ as a living person. This 'devotion to Christ' which he had learned from his fellow-ascetics was his main weapon in the fight. In time of temptation he invoked Christ's name and the demon fled. At times he suffered severe temptations against purity, but 'putting Christ in his heart, he put out the fire of passion.'[6] On his return to the tomb he challenged the demons: 'Here I am,' he said, 'Nothing will ever separate me from the love of Christ'. On another occasion the demons multiplied their attacks. Antony was deeply distressed and cried in vain to the Lord who seemed to be far remote. Yet he did his best and stood his ground courageously. When the trial was over, the light of Christ shone again. Antony asked reproachfully: 'Where were you, Lord? Why did you not come at once to put an end to my pain?' 'Antony, I was here all the time,' was the reply, 'I was watching the contest. Since you stood firm and did not yield, I shall always be your help.'[7]

In intimate friendship with Jesus, Antony found the source of constant joy. Afterwards he used to say to his disciples:

don't be downcast as if you were going to your death. Rather be of good courage and rejoice always as men who are being saved. Remember that the Lord is with us. If our enemies find us joyful in the Lord, ever mindful that everything is in His hands, they will turn tail ... We must always consider the things of the Lord, and let our souls always rejoice in hope.[8]

The fort in the desert

Antony was thirty-five. Urged by 'greater zeal for the service of God' and acting on the advice of his old spiritual father, he went forth into the solitude of the desert. He crossed the Nile, and settled on its eastern bank at Pispir. There he shut himself up in a deserted fort where bread was brought to him twice a year. In Scripture the desert is the setting of the theophanies, and in the fort where 'he trained himself for a long time,' he entered upon a new paschal combat.[9]

The contest took place at a deeper level than the first struggle against the passions. In prolonged silent prayer Antony purified his heart and entered into intimacy with God. The demons were still at hand ready to discourage him, but he meditated on Scripture, sang psalms, worked with his hands, and strove to surrender himself ever more completely into God's hands, trusting in His love for men.

When after twenty years his friends broke down the door and forced Antony to show himself, he emerged 'as from some inmost shrine, initiated into the mysteries and God-born'. This passage is one of the most famous pages in monastic literature. In carefully chosen phrases, Athanasius set out to present Antony as 'perfect', as one who through intimacy with God had achieved an ideal, comprehensible both to pagan and Christian alike. The perfect balance of his body was but a mirror of his soul:

His friends marvelled at seeing him neither corpulent from lack of exercise, nor emaciated from fasting and his war against the demons. Spiritually pure, he was neither disheartened by sadness nor dissipated by pleasure, neither dejected nor jubilant. The sight of the crowd did not elate him nor did their greeting embarrass him. He was completely controlled, a man of perfect equilibrium, as one governed by reason and keeping himself in his natural condition.[10]

In the words of Athanasius, the 'natural condition' is the state of man before original sin. Clement and Origen had given the name of *apatheia* to this perfect balance and self-mastery and considered it the necessary condition for any intimate union with God. This idea was to occupy the minds of many later monastic authors. Antony had already progressed far on the spiritual path.

Antony broadens his spiritual fatherhood

Purified and filled with the strength of the Spirit, Antony's soul was now restored to its 'natural condition' in the image of God. From this time on the saint was able to radiate God's peace to others and became the spiritual father of the great numbers who flocked to see him.

> He could be distinguished from his brethren because he was never agitated, never gloomy, for his soul was serene and his mind full of joy.[11] Simply from observing his manner of life, many strove to imitate him.[12]

Antony made use of his charism to console the afflicted and so became 'the spiritual doctor of Egypt'. Lay people, monks and clergy crowded to consult him, and the Emperor himself wrote for spiritual advice.[13] He was full of compassion for every kind of suffering, and did not hesitate to take long journeys or to approach officials to help the poor or those who suffered injustice. As the request of the bishops, he even travelled once to Alexandria to confute the Arians, who had asserted that Antony was following their sect.[14]

He had already been there of his own accord. When, under fresh persecution,[15] Christians were being arrested and taken to Alexandria, Antony and a group of monks followed in their train to serve and encourage them. They thus exposed themselves to martyrdom, but neither he nor they were accorded this grace. When the persecution was over, Antony returned to his cell to resume more fervently than ever his life of mortification, for God had chosen him to be a 'martyr (i.e. a witness) of conscience.'[16]

The inner mountain

All this activity in the world must not be allowed to conceal the other side of the picture. Antony spent the greater part of his time in solitude, occupied in prayer, manual work and the struggle against temptation. Day after day he persevered in his life of penance, striving to make progress as if he were a mere beginner.[17] In the desert Antony was conscious of waging war on behalf of the whole world, and when he strove to grow in intimacy with God, he bore with him all souls of goodwill. His object in recommending manual work to his disciples was that 'monks should not be a burden to anyone and should help the poor and needy by the sweat of their brow.' (Syriac version) The Greek version (*Ch. 44*) gives manual work an additional value – 'to preserve love and harmony among the brethren.' Antony's external labours thus shed a new light on the prayer of the solitary. In his heart, love for God and love for men could not be separated.

For a long time he tried to find a practical solution to the problem of fulfilling this twofold duty. At first he tried to 'set a period of time during which he would neither go out himself nor receive anyone', but people pressed round and 'very many sufferers slept outside his cell'.

Finally, under God's inspiration, 'fearing to become proud of the works God was doing through his hands', he took to flight once again. This time he penetrated further into the deep desert near the Red Sea, beyond the reach of man.[18] His flight, however, did not proceed from selfishness. Every three weeks or so he would return to a more accessible spot, where people could consult him.[19] In addition, he continued to make long journeys to visit his disciples scattered throughout the desert; making his way back as soon as possible to his beloved solitude. To an army officer who begged him to stay with him a little longer, Antony explained: 'Just as fish die, when on dry land, so monks grow lax when they loiter or dally with the world. Therefore, monks must be off to the mountain as fish to the sea. If they dawdle they lose sight of the interior life.'[20] One day Abba Antony received a letter from the Emperor Constantius inviting him to Constantinople. He was uncertain what to do. 'Should I go?' he asked Abba Paul, his disciple. 'If you go,' Paul replied, 'you will be called Antony; if you don't go, Abba Antony.'[21] In other words, 'if you go, you will forfeit your spiritual fatherhood.'

After a last visit to most of his disciples, he returned and announced to his two companions that his end was near. With his face filled with joy, he died in peace a week later at the age of one hundred and five years, in the year A.D. 356.

Bishop Athanasius, his friend, wrote his life 'for the utility of all, that the brethren may learn what the life of a monk should be.'[22]

Father of Christian monks and their model

We shall understand more fully the ideal that St Athanasius wanted to put before Christian monks if we single out the essential features of Antony's monasticism. The mainspring of his existence was his search for God; hence those flights into the desert that punctuate the external life of the saint, and are clearly seen as longings for greater intimacy with God by the rejection of all that could hinder this union.

The fruit of this striving was the marvellous poise he attained and the joy that radiated from him. The appearance of Antony as he emerged from the fort bears graphic witness to his complete and perfect submission to the divine presence which entered him and restored him to the 'natural state',[23] of intimacy with God. The reflection on the Divine, brings about healing of soul and body, but at the same time draws the saint to deeper silence and an ever more profound contemplation of the 'Kingdom of God that is within us'.[24]

The Life describes in detail the means used to attain this end, but we can sum them up briefly as love, which urges the soul to imitate Christ, and struggle against everything that impedes intimacy with Him.

The principal obstacles are first the passions, which must be mastered and then the demon, who begins by trying to tempt the soul with evil thoughts and later seems to assume visible form.[25]

The chief weapons in the fight are suited to the object of the struggle; the first is love of Christ, shown by imitating His virtues, in particular the virtues of faith, humility and gentleness; the second is asceticism, whereby purity of heart is attained through bodily mortification and strict control over the mind. Manual labour is of great help in achieving this twofold aim, because it tires the body and makes the mind better able to concentrate.

All these efforts would be futile without God's help and this must be sought in prayer. The prayer itself, made privately or in common, assists the soul in its ascent to God, where it finds its dwelling place. Equal importance is attached to reading and meditation on Holy Scripture, for it enriches the mind with an inexhaustible treasure of holy thoughts and keeps it directed to God. It is useful to learn long passages by heart, particularly the Psalms.

Antony's flight into solitude did not proceed from selfishness. His work was undertaken 'to help the poor';[26] his prayer was on behalf of the whole Church and his silence so filled him with the Spirit of God that he became 'the spiritual physician of Egypt'.[27]

Notes

1 The quotations from the Life of St Antony are indicated by V.A. followed by the number of the chapter given according to the translation of R.T. Meyer in *Ancient Christian Writers* No. 10.
2 V.A. 16, see also 3, 7, 19, 55, 91.
3 V.A. 2.
4 V.A. 3–4.
5 V.A. 9.
6 V.A. 5.
7 V.A. 9.
8 V.A. 42.
9 V.A. 12.
10 V.A. 14.
11 V.A. 67.
12 V.A. 44, 14.

13 V.A. 81.
14 V.A. 69.
15 Persecution of the Emperor Maximin Daja about 311. V.A. 46.
16 V.A. 47
17 'Every day he began afresh, counting for nothing the time past, but regarding himself as having only just begun to serve God and striving to make himself worthy to present himself before God' V.A. 91, see also 7, 17.
18 V.A. 49–50
19 V.A. 84–85.
20 V.A. 85.
21 Apothegm. Antony 31; V.A. 81.
22 V.A. Prologue.
23 V.A. 20.
24 V.A. 20.
25 V.A. 3, 19, 30.
26 V.A. 3.
27 V.A. 87.

CHAPTER IV

St Pachomius and his Disciples Theodore and Orsisius

The life of Pachomius

During Antony's lifetime monks grouped themselves either in semi-eremitical centres or in regular communities. One of the most highly organized types of monastic cenobitism that has ever existed was created at this time. This was the achievement of Pachomius, a young pagan, led to Christ by the charity of Christian villagers in helping destitute prisoners.

It was the year 313 and Pachomius was twenty. Though not physically robust, he had been coerced, with all the other youths of his village, into the army of the Emperor Maximinus for the war against Licinius. The conscripts were being brought down the Nile, halting at night in military camps and prisons.

At the prison of Antinoe, Christians of the neighbourhood came and offered food and drink to the poor lads who were without both. Pachomius asked his companions the reason for this unexpected comfort. 'They are Christians', was the reply, 'and they treat us kindly for the sake of the God of Heaven'. Drawing apart, he spent the whole of that night in prayer. 'Lord Jesus Christ, God of all saints,' he said, 'May your kindness reach me soon; save me from this affliction and, in return, I will serve mankind all the days of my life.'[1]

Within a few days news arrived of the defeat of Maximinus. The conscripts were released and Pachomius sought baptism at the Christian village of Chenobosia, not far from his birthplace, Latopolis, near Thebes.

After baptism, he devoted some months to serving the poor and did social work in the village. Feeling that such work was rather the duty of the clergy[2] and interfered with his growing desire for a life dedicated to prayer, he entrusted his commitments to a worthy man and betook himself to Palamon, an aged anchorite, to be trained in the monastic life.

Palamon gave him the *schema* or monastic habit, and taught him:

> according to the monastic rule received from his predecessors ... to keep vigil, to recite God's word, to work with his hands for his bodily needs and to distribute any surplus to the poor; to fast daily until evening during the summer, and every two or three days in winter.[3]

One day, as Pachomius was wandering in the desert, praying and collecting brushwood for a fire, he came to a deserted village called Tabennesis where, during prayer, he was inspired to lay the foundation of a monastery. Palamon assisted him to build a cell there, and they visited each other in turn until Palamon's death a few months later. When others joined him, Pachomius understood that his vocation was 'to minister to the race of men and reconcile them to God'. He trained them by example rather than by precept, himself preparing the table, working in the garden, tending the sick. The principal request he made was that his followers should study and reflect on the Bible, especially the Gospels and the Psalms.

Soon other disciples came, but along with increase in numbers came troubles. Pachomius was obliged to expel certain monks who refused to obey and showed 'a worldly spirit', but, supported by the local bishop, he restored peace and the brethren reached several hundreds in number. Among the new arrivals was a boy of fourteen, named Theodore, whom Pachomius later made his assistant.

At the same time the organization of the monastery began to take shape. The general plan was perhaps inspired by the military camps Pachomius had visited in his youth, with enclosure wall, gatehouse, kitchen, refectory, hospital; but the brethren were divided into tribes and houses perhaps after the manner of the Israelites. Each house had a common room for prayer, instructions and other communal activities, and separate rooms for the monks. There was a special house for the postulants, others were set aside for particular trades, and the daily routine of the monastery was assured by the less specialized. Outside the enclosure the monks practised agriculture, and inside, devoted themselves to making ropes, mats and baskets.

Pachomius built a church in the village which at first was used by monks and faithful alike, but as both increased in numbers, he built a separate monastic church. To preserve humility, he refused to allow his monks to be ordained nor did he become a priest himself. The parish priest celebrated Mass on Saturday evenings in the village and in the monastery on Sunday mornings.

A nunnery was also built at some distance, ruled over by Mary, Pachomius' sister. A wise senior monk was appointed to advise the nuns and act as intermediary with the monks.

Within a short time, the growing numbers of monks forced him to make several foundations, at first in desert villages nearby. One of these, at Pvoou or Faou, became a few years later the chief house of the Pachomian monks. In the course of time other houses were founded farther afield both to the North and South.

The founder was thus at the head of a kind of Congregation of many monasteries and thousands of monks. He entrusted the practical organization of each house to a superior or steward under the supervision of a general bursar residing with him at Faou. General meetings were held there twice a year, one at Easter and the other in August, for the audit and the appointment of new superiors.

Pachomius and his successors spent most of their time visiting the various houses to instruct the brethren. As his Life tells us, 'He was a shepherd close to the great Good Shepherd, Christ. He frequently travelled from monastery to monastery to visit the brothers, admonishing them by the word of God, caring for them like a nursing mother warming her children by the love in her heart.'[4] The monastic timetable provided for several weekly instructions by the steward or master of the house – two on Sundays, one on Wednesdays, Fridays and Saturdays. There are vivid accounts of some of these talks given by Pachomius or Theodore to hundreds of the brethren, sometimes gathered indoors, sometimes in the open air under palm trees.

The subject of the talks, especially those of Pachomius was based on Scripture from which he took texts as themes for meditation on dogma. He drew from the Scriptures likewise for his Rule, a body of *Precepts* with three short addenda.[5] The complete Rule seems to have been built up gradually for the instruction of the fervent and the control of the unruly. Even if Scripture was not always quoted, it was nevertheless the true source of Pachomius' life, as Antony attested when he heard of his death: 'I have often heard tell how truly your father conducted his life according to the Holy Scriptures.'

Pachomius made mutual obedience and fraternal charity the corner-stones of his Rule, and considered his own office of Superior as a 'service of all'. On visiting a monastery, he placed himself as a simple monk under a house-master and shared in the hardest manual labour. He carried on his shoulders bundles of reeds from the river and brought them to the monastery, built walls, cleaned out the bottoms of wells ... All these are noted incidentally in the recorded anecdotes of his life.

Other information about his personal life indicates that he went through the same stages of spiritual growth as Antony. His initial struggles against his passions for self-mastery, were followed by a more open contest with the devil, till finally filled with the Holy Spirit, he received the charism of guiding others.

St Pachomius died in 346, ten years before St Antony, a victim of the plague which decimated his monastery.

Theodore and Orsisius

A few years before his death, Pachomius deprived his assistant, Theodore, of the right of succession. Theodore was a

good monk, a brilliant teacher, a practical organizer, but a
man possibly lacking in the spirit of monastic simplicity.
The first successor of Pachomius died soon after his elec-
tion, and a young man, Orsisius, was chosen in his place.
He met with powerful opposition from elder superiors who
were jealous of their independence. As a last resort, he
appealed for help to Theodore and joined with him in the
government of the Congregation. Order was gradually re-
established, perhaps only too well. The monasteries grew
rich, and the monks lost their fervour in the fever of trade.
Theodore recognized the deterioration but was powerless to
repair it. He asked leave of Orsisius to retire and died soon
after, imploring God with all his heart for the amendment
of the Congregation.

Orsisius, now in a firmer position, laboured valiantly to
remedy the situation. He visited the monasteries, exhorted
the brethren and wrote letters to the superiors, which are
still esteemed, but after his death the Congregation
collapsed under the weight of material interests, fresh divisions, and failure of the religious spirit.

The Spirituality of Pachomius

Scripture and the Rule

Scripture took first place. The monks were required to
meditate on it constantly and learn it by heart. In spite of
their conciseness many prescriptions of the Rule were based
on the Bible,[6] and they believed that the word of God
contained an actual message for every monk. Following the
example of its saints – the patriarchs, prophets and apostles
– they also showed themselves as living models of self-
surrender to God. The Rule was thus manifestly a reflection
of Scripture, and its authority derived from the inspired
word of God.

In the eyes of his disciples Pachomius himself was the
spokesman of God and the pre-eminent representative of
the whole monastic tradition, for he had been supremely
successful in applying the riches of the Bible to monastic
life. The Rule was at the same time the adaptation of

Scripture for monks and an epitome of the spiritual experience of the founder and earlier generations of cenobites.

Aims of the monastic life

These aims are clearly shown in the instructions given by Pachomius and Theodore. The monk is a man who strives to live his Christian life to the full. His ideal is the same as that of others – love of God and his neighbour[7] – but he arrives at it by different means, following the Evangelical counsels. The lectures of Theodore, especially the third, advocate renouncement of the world, of marriage and of personal property as the most powerful means of reaching God. Nevertheless, Pachomius did not withdraw from the world out of scorn for other men, but because of 'a charism given from heaven to us miserable creatures.'[8]

The monk aims at salvation and salvation is the same as perfection. It cannot be acquired except through constant effort. 'Profit by the teaching of the Lord, to grow as young plants.'[9] For a monk, this constant struggle is a duty; but he is supported by the example of the saints. The monk must 'travel his earthly path after the manner of the blessed in Heaven and live as the holy angels do.'[10] Perfection is not achieved here below in some state of *apatheia* or detachment as Clement had thought. For Pachomius as for Antony, the monk must engage in continual warfare to the very end, trusting that God will give Him 'the gift of peace' in this life and in the next, the 'joy of the Kingdom of Heaven'.[11]

The *Koinonia* – the holy community

Obedience is strongly emphasized in the Rule of Pachomius, in his catechesis and in the teaching of his successors, particularly Orsisius. So, too, is the freedom to which the monk is called.[12] But the strong organization of the community is not a rigid framework within which each individual achieves his own salvation. On the contrary, the ruling spirit is one of mutual love, devout, peaceful and supernatural; in this lies the 'communion' of the community. It is the holy *koinonia* defined by Pachomius in the adage: 'May you

profit all as all profit you.'[13] 'The life of the apostles with
the Lord of all' sets the pattern. It is a way of life that
implies a constant striving for good and the renouncement
of material possessions since they are divisive. To cause a
brother sadness is a fault. 'To be in discord with a brother is
to be in a state of hostility to God, and to live in peace with
one's brother is to live in peace with God.' 'Be one in heart
with your brother'.[14] 'Love all men and you will be friend
of Jesus, the friend of men'.[15] Love of God, love of man,
echoes the whole teaching of Scripture and it is on this
foundation that the work of Pachomius is so firmly based.

Notes

1 Translated from *Les Vies Coptes de St. Pachome*, trad. Th. Lefort, p.
   82. We shall quote this book as V.C. The corresponding text in
   English is found in A. Veilleux, *Pachomian Koinonia*, 3 vols.,
   Cistercian Studies 45, henceforth quoted as P.K.
2 The *Pastor of Hermas* considers the care of the poor one of a bishop's
   chief duties. (24. 10th. Mount.) Polycarp also gives much advice to
   the same effect. (Daniélou, *The First Six Hundred Years*, p. 17).
3 V.C. p. 85; P.K.1 p. 31.
4 V.C. p. 119; P.K.1 p. 174.
5 Besides his Rules, Pachomius has left several letters and discourses
   (P.K.2) as well as fragments of catechetical writings. These, as well as
   the letters and catechetical works of his disciples, Theodore and
   Orsisius, have been edited by Th. Lefort in C.S.C.O. 159–60; P.K. 3.
6 In one part of the Rule, however, Pachomius has no hesitation in
   finding inspiration in the learned writings of a pagan Egyptian cult:
   (cf. Th. Lefort, 'St. Pachome et Amen-em-ope', in *Museum*, 40 (1927)
   pp. 65–74.
7 Theodore, *Cathechesis*, Lefort, C.S.C.O. 159, pp. 2–20; P.K.2 pp.
   13–41.
8 ibid. C.S.C.O. pp. 41–43; P.K.2, pp. 108–114.
9 ibid. C.S.C.O. p. 23; P.K.3, p. 97.
10 ibid. C.S.C.O. p. 53; P.K.3 p. 109. Pachomius, *Cathechesis*, ibid.
   p. 1; P.K.3 p. 13.
11 Pachomius, *Cathechesis*, ibid. C.S.C.O. p. 2; P.K.3, p. 15; Theodore
   Cathechesis, ibid. C.S.C.O. p. 41; P.K.3 pp. 99; 110.
12 Orsisius, *Testament*, 19; P.K.3 p. 15.
13 Theodore, *Cathechesis*, ibid. C.S.C.O. p. 39; P.K.3 p. 107.
14 Pachomius, *Cathechesis*, ibid. C.S.C.O. p. 15; 2; P.K.3 pp. 29; 14.
15 ibid. C.S.C.O. p. 21; P.K.3, p. 37.

CHAPTER V

The Desert Fathers

The great spiritual fathers and their history

As a true hermit, Antony never had more than one or two brethren dwelling with him, but he had as disciples a number of solitaries with whom he was in regular contact. His Life recounts that:

> he attracted many to the monastic life ... and the desert was peopled with monks who had left their fellow-citizens, to enrol themselves as citizens of heaven.[1]

Many of them have left their mark on history for they have been the source of new developments in monasticism.

Amoun, another rich young man, wished to follow in the same path, but an uncle who was also his tutor forced him to marry. He succeeded in persuading his wife to share with him a life of chastity, but only after eighteen years would she consent to his leaving her to build a cell 'in the Mountain of Nitria'. This 'Mountain' consisted of a region of small hills at the edge of the Western desert towards the Delta. From there, he visited her twice a year.

The number of disciples who joined Amoun in this desert was soon so great that many among them began to seek a life of more complete solitude. Faced with this difficulty, Amoun consulted Antony who advised him to found another settlement at a distance of half a day's walk in the desert, where the cells would be so scattered that each would be out of earshot of the other. Hence the place was simply called 'The Cells'. Among these groups of monks, a certain amount of organization gradually appeared. There were places for hermits, for others living in two's and three's and for communities numbering hundreds. Nitria was considered as a training centre from which those with a vocation passed on to an eremitical life in the desert of the 'Cells'. There, as at Nitria, the centre of the settlement was the church where the monks assembled for the Eucharist on Saturday and Sunday. Communion was taken to each, every day.

Seven bakeries supplied the bread for Nitria and for the 'Cells'. Various industries were carried on, especially the making of ropes and cloth. There was a hospital staffed with doctors, a garden and a guest-house where visitors were offered free hospitality for a week. If they wished to stay longer they had to work. Some remained several years without ever becoming monks, though, in a sense, they formed part of the community and were subject to suitable discipline, as the following detail in the history naïvely demonstrates. In the middle of the courtyard stood three palm trees, on which hung three whips – one to punish faults committed by monks, one for thieves and the third for guests. We must not forget that at that period corporal punishment gave no more offence than would a rebuke or a fine in our day.

The communities at Nitria and the 'Cells' were guided by a college of priests (eight at the time when Palladius visited them). The most senior among them was responsible for the liturgy, conferences and the administration of justice.

Macarius the Egyptian, another imitator of Antony, embarked on his ascetical life in a village and later moved to the desert about the time that Amoun went to Nitria. He settled in Scete, forty miles to the south and was followed by others. One of their first problems was that of the Eucharist. Macarius used to travel to Nitria for Mass, but the forty miles on foot in the desert was beyond the strength of most monks even in those days. So it came about that, acting on Antony's advice, Macarius consented to be ordained priest.

Macarius was certainly a great spiritual master. Many letters and homilies have been attributed to him. One among those that seems most likely to be authentic – *the Epistle to the Sons of God* – contains a beautiful chapter on humility comparable to what St Benedict and St Bernard have written on this subject.

The most famous of the Desert Fathers lived at Nitria, the 'Cells' and Scete. Pior, Pambo, Or, Macarius of Alexandria and later, Evagrius lived at Nitria. Arsenius, Moses, Amoes, John 'Colobos' (the dwarf), Isidore and Paphnutius, lived at the 'Cells' and at Scete. Here also lived Poemen, who was probably the first to collect the 'Sayings of the Fathers' the *Apophthegmata Patrum*. The wisdom and virile spirituality that informs these has been a source of inspiration for monastic life down to our own day.

The *Apophthegmata* constitute one of the principal sources of our knowledge of these famous hermits. The collection was put together piecemeal at a time when life in the desert was being rendered hazardous by the political conditions prevailing in Egypt, suffering as it was from secular and religious conflicts as well as from Arab incursions. Many monks were massacred, others became lax, and the monastic centres either disappeared or were reduced to a few cells clustered within fortified enclosures. Fearing to lose all the spiritual treasure of the Fathers, some fervent monks wrote down whatever sayings they could remember. The collections thus made were soon grouped into two series, one arranged in alphabetical order, the other according to subject.[2]

Famous visitors also have left us accounts of their encounters with the Egyptian monks – Palladius in his *Lausiac History*, Cassian in his *Institutes* and *Conferences*, and an unknown monk who wrote a work called *The History of the Monks of Egypt*, which Rufinus translated. Finally, St Jerome played his part by translating several of the lives, in particular, that of the first hermit, St Paul.

The spirituality of the desert

The spirituality of the desert admitted of several contradictory positions, a sign of the tensions already existing in monastic life. Withdrawal from the world is represented by

Abbot Arsenius, at one time tutor to the Emperor's sons, an austere and silent man, keeping his door closed to visitors, adopting a motto re-echoed through the whole East: 'Flee, be silent, be at peace.' In contrast with him we have Abbot Moses, a former brigand, a dark-skinned Ethiopian, tall and slender, whose hospitality was legend. He always greeted visitors with a comforting smile of welcome. To a brother who said, when taking leave, 'Forgive me, Father, for I have impeded you from following your rule,' the old man answered, 'My rule, brother, is to comfort you peacefully when you come, and then to send you away with charity.'[3]

Another aspect of desert spirituality, less wholesome but unfortunately far better known, is demonstrated by Macarius the Alexandrian, a tailor converted at the age of forty, whose vocation seems to have made him eager to outstrip all others in asceticism. So he went for years without cooked food, spent twenty days without sleep, and performed a number of other exploits of this nature. This kind of vocation seems to have been particularly evident at the time of the first hermits, the pioneers of the desert, for, a few years later, abnormal asceticism was generally discouraged and the 'Sayings' often praise moderation. Abbot Poemen used to say, 'All that exceeds the normal comes from the devil.'[4]

The Desert Fathers specialized in studying the passions of the human heart and the way to combat them so as to reach union with God.[5] The reality of this struggle and the necessity for it played such a part in their lives that often, following St Paul's example,[6] they described monks as soldiers or athletes. Palladius calls the two SS Macarius 'invincible athletes'.[7] As a motive for breaking silence, Rufinus gives: 'To anoint with the comfort of salutary counsel the athletes chosen for the combat.'[8] St Jerome calls Paul and Antony 'soldiers of Christ', and introduces the history of the monk, Malchus, with these rousing words: 'See how a man consecrated to God can die but cannot be vanquished'.[9] Athanasius, Basil, the Cappadocian Fathers, and Cassian use similar terms.

These analogies are made so consistently and seriously

that we are convinced they are not used simply as a literary device. For athletes of Christ, the struggle was seen as a vital necessity. After Abbot John Colobos had learnt how to control his passions, he prayed that God would give him something more to strive for, 'because it is in fighting that the soul makes progress'.[10] Antony expressed the same idea in an even more radical way: 'The monk who has not been tried cannot enter the Kingdom of Heaven. In fact, if you do away with temptation, no-one can be saved'.[11] Others asserted that temptation was the test of faith and of our love for Christ; the narrow way. They supported their claim by citing Acts (*14, 22*) 'Through many tribulations we must enter into the Kingdom of God.' Struggle strengthens the soul 'as fire hardens brick'.[12] Through suffering and trials a man is made aware of his weakness and of the help God gives him.[13] Trials also make known to a man his hidden passions,[14] and help him to purify himself from them, acquiring on the way humility and the habit of prayer.[15] So it is normal that trials continue throughout life. Antony used to repeat this constantly to his disciples; many of the Fathers who followed him reiterated the same idea in different ways.[16] Abbot John Colobos sums it up admirably in his definition of a monk: 'What is being a monk? Doing battle'.[17]

The Soldiers of Christ did not go to the desert to flee from the difficulties of the world but, on the contrary, to fight the enemy of the Church, the devil, on his own ground, in a personal struggle, as Christ himself had done. It was in solitude that the demon's action in the soul was more clearly manifested, for, as St Basil aptly said: 'If he does not create our evil dispositions, he at least makes use of them.'[18] He strives to nourish the passion to which he sees we are inclined. Macarius saw him in the form of a merchant of quack medicines, laden with little bottles, offering the monks one after the other until he found one that they liked.[19]

But the attitude of the Fathers towards the devil was primarily one of bold realism.[20] For all his aggressiveness he was weak, ignorant of the real nature of the soul and of God, whose angels keep watch beside us. Christ, like a fair adjudicator in the stadium, permits no unequal combat.

Many of the monks even went so far as to provoke the devil openly and make fun of him. When St Antony saw him appear in the form of ferocious and menacing beasts, he said: 'If you really had any power to harm, just one of you would have been enough.'[21] Later, Isaac the Syrian differentiates four principal ways in which the devil tempts man: he tries to overcome the feeble by violent assaults as soon as they enter religious life. With the more courageous he waits for a moment of relaxation or abatement of fervour. Some he tries to subdue by making them proud of whatever good they have accomplished; and lastly he has recourse to the demands of human nature – money and sex.[22]

The monk must counter these temptations by combat, 'striving lawfully,' as St Paul says (*2 Tim. 2–5*) in a passage often quoted by Cassian. That is to say, the first reaction must be prayer. Many borrow a metaphor from Psalm 136: 'Break evil thoughts into pieces on Christ, as soon as they arise.'[23] Others speak of crying out to God or fleeing to Him, as a man chased by a wild beast climbs a tree to escape.[24] All agree that it is better not to offer direct resistance to temptation but to cut it short by 'pouring prayer upon it as water on a fire.[25] All these efforts, however, must be accompanied by a striving to obtain self-mastery for, as Abbot-Pityrion says: 'A man who wants to put the devil to flight must first control his passions.'[26]

Indeed all the Fathers insist that one of the chief conditions for success in the fight is to be on the alert. The collections of 'Sayings' all devote a chapter to this subject. One must watch the thoughts that enter the mind because 'every sin begins with a thought.'[27] The Apophthegmata multiply comparisons to bring home this point. We must examine our thoughts as soldiers on guard at the town gates have to distinguish friend from foe, or as man chases the birds that attack his crops.[28] A rat cannot get at the wick of a lamp that is lit, but if the light is out, it drags it over and the lamp shatters on the ground.[29] Vigilance is necessary against danger from without as well as from within, says Amma Syncletica, for windows must be closed to keep out dust and thieves, and boats can capsize through the action of the waves as easily as through a small leak in the hull.[30]

Negligence leads to tepidity, to lack of charity and little
by little, to serious faults, for 'the beginning of all evil is to
allow it to enter the mind'.[31] It gives rise also to dissipation,
to excessive freedom in words and conduct that, like the
wind coming from the desert, dries up the fruits of virtue, or
a fire that destroys dry reeds.[32]

Here also a prompt reaction is essential to drive away the
first thought of sin or any desire for it. Just as young plants
are easier to pull out than those that are firmly rooted, so it
is with newly begun practices.[33] Sometimes the remedy is to
fly from the danger; 'the fish cannot stop the angler throw-
ing the hook, but it can swim away,' and one of the devil's
tricks is to blind us by some illusion so that we do not see
the snare.[34]

Once a passion has been conquered, one must take care
not to fall again because a single action is enough to
reawaken an old habit.[35] But if one does fall, one must get
up again, steadfastly trusting in God. Abbot Poemen
advises the monk to cast his faults down before the Lord,[36]
not allowing himself to be overcome by temptation but
persevering in hope and trust in God,[37] without worrying
about the future, but making a fresh beginning each day.[38]

All the collections of 'Sayings' have chapters on patience
and strength, with numerous encouragements to perseverance. Amma Sara, who had to fight for thirteen years
against a temptation to fornication, used simply to say: 'O
my God, give me strength'.[39] In times of trouble there must
be no relaxation in the daily duties or imagining that one
would do better in another place. Once an irritable monk
went off to the desert, thinking to find peace in solitude, but
when his pitcher happened to overturn he smashed it in
anger.[40]

A little relaxation is sometimes necessary[41] but it must not
prove an obstacle to perseverance: 'Drink, eat and sleep, but
do not leave your cell.' 'Trees that are often transplanted do
not bear fruit ... and eggs left alone produce no chickens.'[42]

At a deeper level, this steadfastness is essentially an effort
to fill the mind with strengthening thoughts. Meditation on
the Scriptures, recollection of past fervour and of the troubles of others keep the attention occupied, lead to God and,

by the same token, drive away unwholesome ideas.[43] It is also helpful to open one's heart to a spiritual Father who can guide and cure the soul.[44] The 'Sayings' could be summed up as the answers of the Fathers to monks coming to them with their difficulties.

These wise directors were aware that the passions are linked with each other and react on our faculties and on our bodies. Evagrius and, later, Cassian were to develop this teaching, distinguishing eight principal passions which give rise to the seven capital sins. But each passion has its own particular cause. Some, like gluttony and impurity, involve participation of the body and require control over one's thoughts and bodily asceticism.[45] Envy and anger spring from external causes. One must attack them with vigour at the outset, by meditation on Scripture, by manual work and by peaceful contemplation.[46] What seems the negative task of denying the passions must be done 'with intelligence', that is to say, it must be adapted to individual souls and must be accompanied by positive development of virtues.[47] The twofold presence in us of a tendency to evil and a desire to do good is expressed by the virtue of compunction or *penthos*, which as Abbot Pastor says: 'has a double function; it fosters and it safeguards.'[48] It is a return to God through fear, which ends in love.[49]

It is indeed towards this love, expressed by prayer as unceasing as possible, that the 'Desert Fathers' strove. They were very reticent about their mystical experiences, the manifestations of which they tried to hide from their disciples, but their constant effort to keep their hearts attentive to God is clearly apparent. All could have said with Abba Lucius:

> With God's help I sit down and make ropes, saying, 'Have pity on me, Lord, according to your great mercy' ... I spend the whole day working and praying, silently or aloud.[50]

The closer one drew to God, the simpler the prayer, till it became a single act of love and confidence. 'Abba Macarius, when asked about his method of praying, answered:

Many words are not needed in prayer, but we often stretch out our hands and say, 'Lord, have pity on me, according to your will and your power.' When your soul is in any difficulty, say 'Help me', and God has mercy because He knows what is best for you.[51]

Notes

1 V.A. 14.
2 Our quotations are taken from the French translation of the alphabetical series by H. Guy, but we give their number according to the English translation, published in *Cistercian Studies* vol. 59, quoted as Ap.; Helen Waddell also published extracts in 'The Desert Fathers' quoted as H.W. The systematic series is published in French as *Sentences des Pères du Désert*, Ed. Solesmes quoted as S.S. The Syriac version was put into English by W. Budge in *The Paradise of the Fathers*, Vol. II quoted as W.B.II.; B. Ward S.L.G. published the Greek alphabetical collection in *The Sayings of the Desert Fathers* and the Systematic Collection in *The Wisdom of the Desert Fathers*. An excellent epitome of the *Apophthegmata* was made in the Middle Ages by the Spanish bishop, Martin of Dumes, published by Helen Waddell. Lastly, we find an echo of the Desert Fathers in the *Philokalia* (Early Fathers of the Philokalia, transl. Kadloubovsky and Palmer) and also in Dorotheus of Gaza, *Cistercian Studies Series 33*, quoted according to S.C. (*Sources Chrétiennes*) 92.
3 Martin of Dumes 28; Ap. Arsenius 2, 7, 8, 28, 38.
4 Ap. Poemen 129. The subject of moderation takes up a whole chapter of the *Apophthegmata*. (S.S.X.). Ap. p. 215. Discretion.
5 Ap. Poemen 8.
6 2 Tim. 2. 3–4, 1 Cor. 9. 24–27.
7 P.L. 73. 761, 35.
8 H.W. p. 76.
9 H.W. p. 39.
10 Ap. J. Colobos (The Dwarf) 13.
11 Ap. Antony 5.
12 Ap. Orsisius 1.
13 Ap. Poemen. 13, 14, 15. *Philocalia*, Mark the ascetic, pp. 65–70. ibid. Isaac of Syria, pp. 62–76.
14 ibid. Isaac of Syria, pp. 215–217; Ap. Syndetica 7.
15 Humility and constant prayer from the headings of chapters of the *Apophthegmata*, SS. 12 and 15; W.B. II pp. 24 and 103. Ap. pp. 216, 217.
16 Ap. Poemen 8, 126, Dorotheus, Inst. 7, No. 401; Ap. Pambo 9.
17 Ap. J. Colobos (The Dwarf), 37.
18 Short Rules 75.
19 Ap. Macarius 3; Matoes 4; Synletica 7. This story is repeated by St

Gregory in his *Life of St Benedict*. Ch. 30.
20 Ap. Poemen 93, 94; Macarius II, 35, 36.
21 V. Ant. ch. 9; Cassian *Inst.* VI ch. 13; Ap. Macarius 13.
22 *Philocalia*, Isaac of Syria pp. 210–214.
23 Martin of Dumes, 3–4.
24 Ap. Macarius Eg. 19; Pachomius P.L. 73, 761, No. 35; 805, No. 203; 806 No. 208; John Colobos (The Dwarf), 12.
25 Ap. Poemen 146; *Philocalia*, Isaac of Syria 55–57, 189.
26 Ap. Pityrion 1; S.S. IV the whole chapter.
27 *Philocalia*, Isaac of Syria 7; W.B. p. 86 No. 386; Ap. Antony 1.
28 W.B. p. 83 No. 370.
29 S.S. XI 43, 50, 79; Ap. Orsisios 2.
30 S.S. XI 33–34. Ap. Syncletica 23–24.
31 *Philocalia*, St Mark, the ascetic, P. 71, S.S. XI, 47.
32 Dorotheus of Gaza *Inst.* IV, No. 52–53.
33 W.B. II pp. 81–82; No. 360, 362, 363. *Philocalia*, pp. 138–141, 180; Dorotheus of Gaza, p. 56; P.L. 73, 761, 35.
34 Ap. J. Guy *Dialogue des Vieillards* 18; Ap. Sarmatas 5; John Colobos (The Dwarf) 5–6; Poemen 59.
35 Dorotheus of Gaza Inst. XI pp. 123–173.
36 Ap. Poemen 123–125.
37 Ap. Poemen 85, 93, 102.
38 Ap. Poemen 85–126, W.B. II p. 86 No. 385; Ap. Sisoes 22–38; W.B. II p. 159 Nos. 362–363.
39 S.S. VII; Ap. Sara, 1–2; cf. p. 214; J. Guy *Anonymous* No. 75, 76, 77; Orsisius 1; W.B. p. 47, No.2.
40 S.S. VII, 33; H.W. p. 126 VII. No.33; Ap. Isidore 4.
41 Ap. Antony 13; S.S. IV, 2, Ap. Poemen 184.
42 S.S. VII. 15; Ap. Heraclides 1; Syncletica 6.
43 Ap. Poemen 125; Epiphanius 3, 6, 7; Syncletica 27; *Philocalia* Antony p. 27; Isaac of Syria, 18–19.
44 P.L. 73, 745, 13; Ap. Moses, 1; John Colobos (The dwarf) 18; Poemen 93.
45 P.L. 73, 742, 47; 745–13; Ap. Syncletica 2, 3, 4, 5, 6, Sara, 1–2. Cassian *Institutes* Bk VI–XII, Conf. V.
46 P.L. 73, 780, 104–105; Ap. Syncletica 23, 27; Isidore, 2, 3, 5; Poemen 69, 103, 168; [J. Budge; Anonymous 63].
47 Joseph 3; James 4. John Colobos (The Dwarf) 34; Poemen 22, 109, 119.
48 Ap. Poemen 39.
49 The chapter of Apophthegmata on compunction shows clearly this complexity. S.S. III. Ap. p. 213. See also Hauserr, *Penthos*.
50 Ap. Lucius I.
51 Ap. Macarius of Egypt 19; S.S. III, 10.

CHAPTER VI

Monachism in Syria and Palestine from the first to the fifth century

IN SYRIA

Syrian monachism has always had its own individual character. One of the most striking was the practice of extreme penance,[1] such as wearing chains or spending one's whole life under a tree or on top of a column after the example of St Simeon Stylites. But we know from the lives of these monks, written by Theodoret of Cyrus in his *Historia Religiosa*, that these practices were not regarded by contemporaries as eccentric but, on the contrary, were completely in line with local tendencies. These people really had a predilection for deep-rooted asceticism, perhaps brought to them by Hindu monks, many of whose habitual practices we find also in Syria, in particular the custom of monks living as beggars and wanderers.

The influence of the monks of Egypt and Cappadocia soon began to be felt, but from the beginning, Syrian monachism preserved its insistence on personal prayer, the 'taste of God' present in the depths of the heart. From this milieu also came monks who count among the most cultured and sensitive writers of the Eastern Church. The foremost among these was St Ephrem, poet and liturgist, who showed clearly the essentials of monastic life.

St Ephrem

St Ephrem was born in Nisibis in Mesopotamia in A.D. 306[2]

He became deacon of the town and directed a school similar to that run by Origen. When the Persians invaded the region in 363, he fled to Edessa where he stayed till his death in 373. His monastic teaching was developed principally in his *Carmina Nisibena*, a eulogy of three bishops of Nisibis whom he had known: James, when he was a child, Babu, as a young man, Vologese, in his maturity. Interesting vignettes can be found also in his *Commentary on the Gospel Concordant*, his hymns and his *De Virginitate*.

He laid little stress on the external forms of monastic life though he praised eremiticism,[3] considering it the highest state for a monk, he seemed to have belonged to a period when ascetics who sought perfection alone or in groups were not yet clearly recognized as a special category in the Church. St Ephrem was more attracted by monastic virtues than by its institutions.

For him the principal virtue for a monk was sincerity. One should be a monk outwardly, but still more in the heart. He would give thirty marks to one for fasting, sixty to one for charity and a hundred to one for truth.[4]

He held virginity to be the highest level of Christian life. It is a special vocation, implying a striving for perfection and a willingness to bear one's cross. The beggar, Lazarus, is a symbol of it.[5] Virginity is equivalent to martyrdom if it is accompanied by careful watch over thoughts, desires and actions. Through virginity, love for many souls replaces love for one woman.[6] The cloister alone does not suffice as a safeguard for it; it must be sustained by mortification of body and soul.[7]

Poverty is more important than bodily mortification. St Ephrem cites the example of the bishops of Nisibis, who possessed nothing whatever, their whole treasure being the Church.[8] For St Ephrem, asceticism was no more than a means to self-mastery, a control of evil thoughts and not the destroying of the God-given beauty of the body.[9]

Ephrem looked on the monk, and especially the hermit, as a man filled with compunction, lamenting sin and doing penance for the sins of others. Through penance a man really 'crucifies sin' and leads sinners to God.[10] The monk's renunciation must be genuine and not mere words. He must be ready to be despised and to die for Christ.[11]

Prayer must be full of faith, taking for its model the prayers of the widow and the publican in the Gospel. It must be firmly grounded on the meditation of Scripture, opening the heart to the word of God which, like a life-giving tree, nourishes it, offering its blessed fruit in abundance.[12] Prayer is crowned by charity which, with its two components, love of God and love of one's neighbour, is like two wings on which man rises up to God.[13]

Since they do not stress the institutional side of monastic life, the writings of St Ephrem have the advantage of under-lining the interior virtues which he considered essential: mastery over the heart and thoughts, detachment from the world, constancy in prayer and meditation on the Scriptures, charity and, above all, sincerity; all outward acts must be an expression of the state within.

Itinerant monks

Another aspect of Syrian monachism was the practice of leaving one's country out of love for God. The idea perhaps came from Hindu travelling monks, but it corresponded, too, with the nature of the country, at the crossroads between Asia and the Western world and an important centre on the caravan routes. The practice was encouraged also by the persecutions that periodically forced Christians to take to flight and hide. The monks followed the cara-vans, preaching and founding churches in all the great trading centres of Asia. They were to be found in Arabia, India, central Asia and even in China. Moreover, it is to them that we owe the introduction of monastic life into Constantinople, around 380.

By its geographical position Syria was also the entry to Palestine for European pilgrims coming from the North. In passing they visited the most famed ascetics. Theodoret speaks of groups of 'Bretons' consulting St Simeon Stylites. It is probably through these pilgrims that Syrian influence was soon to manifest itself among the Celtic monks who, in their turn, were to practise 'the pilgrimage for God'.

PALESTINE

St Chariton

St Chariton,[14] who lived in the third century, filled in Palestine a role similar to that of St Antony in Egypt. Driven by persecution to the Dead Sea desert, he loved the place and lived there as a hermit, attracting to himself a number of disciples. But, since he loved solitude, he confided the care of the new arrivals to an experienced disciple and went further into the desert. Before leaving

> he established a suitable regime for monastic life ... leaving off eating before hunger was satisfied, praying and singing Psalms by day and night, avoiding idleness, the cause of so much evil, and doing manual work, which was to be watered by the holy Psalms.[15]

This grouping of monks was the beginning of a new monastic organization – the 'Laura'.

The steep sides of the desert were pierced by caves. The largest served as a chapel; in others the monks lived during their noviciate. Deeper in the desert dwelt the solitaries who came to the centre for the Sunday liturgy and to exchange the products of their week's labour for provisions for their simple meals and for the materials necessary to carry on their work of making mats and ropes.

St Euthymius

During the early years of the fifth century, Euthymius, a young priest of Melitene on the Euphrates, went on a pilgrimage to Jerusalem and entered the Laura of St Chariton where he became superior. He introduced the custom of going into the desert from the octave of the Epiphany until Palm Sunday.

Following the example of St Chariton, Euthymius left the care of training the novices to his disciple, Theoctistus and went himself into the desert. There he encountered an important Arab tribe and converted them. They needed a priest, so, seeing the seriousness of their faith, Euthymius ordained the chief of the tribe, Aspebet (Peter). This man was later to play a prominent part at the Council of Ephesus. His brother-in-law, Mares, became a monk and later was one of the successors of Euthymius.

When the See of Jerusalem was for a time occupied by an anti-Chalcedon bishop, Euthymius was obliged to go farther south into the desert. There a disciple named Gerontius joined him. This man later founded another type of monastery in the plain of Jericho. Instead of having only the noviciate at the centre, he established a cenobium taking care, however, that those who had the right vocation for it should have the opportunity of living an eremitical life, as in the Laura.

At his death in 473, Euthymius asked that his Laura might follow the new model with a cenobium at the centre.

St Sabas

In 456, a young man from Cappadocia presented himself at the Laura of Euthymius. He was called Sabas and he had fled from his home. After proving his vocation, the Abbot sent him back to his parents. In spite of all offers of a good situation, however, Sabas remained firm and was able to return to the Laura. When he was thirty years old he became a hermit and settled in a cave which was the beginning of the 'great Laura', that he founded when disciples joined him. Here there was a large cave, 'a church made by God', to which he added a cenobium, a noviciate and a guesthouse. Later he added other buildings for a group of Armenian monks, who prayed in their own language, and then a large church dedicated to the Mother of God, *Theotokos*. The monastery had dependencies at Jerusalem and Jericho. Here Sabas built a guesthouse and hospital where pilgrims were received without payment.

Life in the monastery was not without its tensions. At one time, Sabas thought it his duty to leave because of a group of malcontents. The bishop made him return and the dissidents departed but not without destroying the monastery tower in their rage. They settled in another house some distance away. Without any bitterness, Sabas went at their request to live with them for several months to help them to build their church and the oven for their bread.

Meanwhile Sabas, at the plea of the monks and the Bishop of Jerusalem, had been ordained priest. The bishop entrusted to him several important missions, in particular to the Emperors Theodosius and Justinian to plead on behalf of the populace. Again retiring to his Laura, he died in 532.

Monasteries at Jerusalem and other holy places

From very early times, monastic colonies had existed in the holy places, especially on Mt Sion and the Mount of Olives. Most of them were formed by foreign pilgrims who had settled there either in cells scattered among the hills or in cenobitic groups of monks or nuns.

Many of these houses were founded by people of high rank who gave up their fortunes to establish monasteries. From Rome came Melanie and her husband who built two monasteries on the Mount of Olives, where important development was made in the liturgy, and another on the site of the Ascension. In 386, Eustochium and Paula established themselves at Bethlehem in a double monastery, where St Jerome lived. In the following century, the Empress Eudoxia retired to Jerusalem (443–460). She founded innumerable monasteries throughout Palestine, but was also the cause of troubles, for she always remained hostile to the ideas and the men of the Council of Chalcedon.[16]

Finally, the region of Gaza must be mentioned. This was always a brilliant intellectual and monastic centre. St Hilarion, a young student of Alexandria recently converted to Christianity, spent some months with Antony. Afterwards, he returned to Gaza, his native land, and established one of the first colonies there. It was a form of monasticism that included both hermits and cenobites. The works of the Pseudo-Denis the Areopagite were written in this milieu, at the end of the fifth or the beginning of the sixth century.

In general, the monasteries of Syria and Palestine show us

an institution, at once adaptable and varied, uniting eremitic and cenobitic forms of life. We have here one of the origins of oriental monachism, but it was to exercise an important influence on the West as well.

Notes

1 On asceticism in Syrian monachism see A. Vööbus: *History of asceticism in the Syrian Orient*, Vol. II, C.S.C.O. 197.
2 cf. 'St Ephrem Moine et Pasteur' by Dom L. Leloir in *Théologie de la Vie Monastique*, ch. IV.
3 *De Virginitate* XXVII.
4 *Carmina Nisibena* XXIX.
5 *Ev. Conc.* XV.
6 *Carm. Nis.* XIX.
7 *Ev. Conc.* VI.
8 *Carm. Nis.* XIX.
9 *Ev. Conc.* VI.
10 *Ev. Conc.* XXI; Carm. Nis. XXI.
11 *Ev. Conc.* X.
12 *Ev. Conc.* I.
13 *Ev. Conc.* XVI.
14 On Palestinian monks see D.J. Chitty: *The Desert a City*.
15 Life of St Chariton: *Acta Sanctorum*, 28 Sept.
16 The Council of Chalcedon defined the doctrine that in Christ there is one person and two natures. This was the cause of long-lasting divisions among the clergy and monks. In general the region round Jerusalem remained faithful to orthodoxy.

CHAPTER VII

St Basil

His life and works

St Basil, born in Cappadocia about 330, studied with great brilliance at Athens and became a teacher of rhetoric in his native town of Caesarea.[1] In 358 under the influence of his elder sister, St Macrina he asked for baptism, renounced his professional career, and began to lead a life of austerity on his property at Annesus on the banks of the River Iris.[2]

He first followed the ideas of Eustathius of Sebaste, but his sound good sense was soon outraged by the exaggerations of his disciples. They wanted to impose the monastic way of life on all Christians, and some of them, deluded by an irrational zeal, fell into excesses of all kinds.[3]

To escape from this difficulty, Basil, decided to undertake a personal study of the New Testament. He published the results in his *Moral Laws*,[4] in which he cited more than 1,500 verses of Scripture, making every effort to adapt them to the needs of his times. This book was not written primarily for monks but for all Christians desiring a life of perfection, such as those who were following the Eustathian movement.

Once he had gained the confidence of these fervent groups, he was often consulted by them, went to visit them and helped them to set up new centres. As a man of action, with much knowledge and influence in different fields, Basil was singled out by the Bishop of Caesarea, who ordained him priest in 370. Soon afterwards he succeeded the bishop, but this did not prevent him from continuing his work of apostleship among the ascetics. Noticing that the same questions were continually being put to him, he wrote out the answers and collected them under the title *Asceticon*.

A first edition, translated into Latin by Rufinus, and called by St Benedict *The Rule of St Basil*, is composed of eleven questions, treated at some length, in which Basil puts forward his own reflections, followed by many short questions posed by the brethren. This book is called the *Small Asceticon*.

Later there appeared a second edition, with fuller development, composed of chapters, wrongly entitled Rules. Supplemented by several introductions, discourses and letters, it forms the *Great Asceticon*.

The early part of the book consists of fifty-five questions or *Longer Rules*. Of these, the first twenty-two develop the eleven questions of the *Small Asceticon*, the rest are new. In the remaining portion, the briefer questions or *Shorter Rules* are increased from 192 in the first edition to 313 in the second. The *Great Asceticon* was translated into Latin in the Middle Ages and was widely distributed among the monasteries of the West as well as of the East.[5]

St Basil also wrote a number of letters, homilies, liturgical and ascetical treatises and theological studies, dealing especially with the Trinity and the Holy Spirit, and defending Catholic doctrine against the Arians. During his stay at Annesus, with the help of his friend, St Gregory Nazianzen, who had come to visit him, he composed a selection of the works of Origen called *Philocalia*.

As bishop, one of Basil's chief aims was to incorporate into the Church the dynamism of the ideas current in his time, at the same time freeing them from any elements of exaggeration or heresy that might be in them. They stemmed from very different sources, some based on a cultured Hellenism and neo-Platonic philosophy,[6] others originating with the austere Syrian ascetics who did not stop short of the wildest extravagances. It was not necessary to stifle their zeal, but on the contrary, he had to create a unity by developing in each:

a desire to please God, at once ardent and insatiable, strong, consistent and unshakable. This disposition is attained by wise and continual contemplation of the grandeur of God, and by constantly bearing in mind and acknowledging all the benefits we have received from Him.[7]

In the same way he strove to resolve the difficulties put in the way of the ascetics by the clergy. The men of the desert thought the priests rich and comfort-loving and were themselves despised in turn for their lack of cleanliness and culture. Basil, therefore, urged those ascetics who were capable of it to become priests, so as to inspire the clergy with their own zeal, and he directed fervent souls towards labours of charity such as hospital work and teaching.

He also reformed the liturgy and so created the Liturgy which bears his name and is still used in many Eastern churches.

His gifts as organizer, theologian and writer have rightly won for him the title 'Basil the Great'. After bravely defending his church against the Arian emperors, he died peacefully in 379.

St Basil and the monastic life

In order to understand the part played by Basil's ascetical writings, one must place them in their historical context. It was believed for a long time that he wrote in reaction to the system of Pachomius, which he considered too rigid. Recent studies have shown that this was not so. Although he had gone to Egypt, it is not certain that he had seen the Pachomian monasteries.[8] His main concern was in other directions. We have seen that he was confronted with the ascetic excesses of the Eustathian movement. Nor had he any need to insist on solitude, virginity, continual prayer and other things of this nature. On the contrary, he had to moderate the fervour of these people by pointing out to them the demands of charity and community life as described in the New Testament. It is to this end that all his efforts were directed and his great merit lies in this constant reference to the charity of Christ and to commonsense.

Another historic aspect to remember is that Basil was not

writing directly for monks but for groups of fervent
Christians. Throughout the development of his writings it is
apparent that only gradually did regular communities
emerge. In the *Morals* we find advice for married people,
for soldiers, for slaves and for the clergy. We must wait for
the additions made in the *Great Asceticon* to the first
edition of the work, to see there evidence of communities
with some kind of organization, a superior and definite
conditions for admission. Still less did he distinguish
between the institutions catering for different religious
vocations.[9] It was natural then that Basil should invite
fervent persons to works connected with the Church, but he
also makes provision for a solitary life devoted almost
entirely to prayer.[10] These men

> contribute to the welfare of their neighbourhood, helping
> by their prayer and penance those who have charge of the
> Church.

The *Morals* already lay down the main lines of Basil's teaching. He insists on good order in the community as is
prescribed in the pastoral epistles, on conduct that
conforms with Christian aims, and on a charity that has its
source in Baptism and the Eucharist.

> What is the true nature of a Christian? By baptism he is
> born of water and by the Holy Spirit born anew. What is
> the true nature of one who is reborn with water? Just as
> Christ died to sin, once for all, so the Christian should die
> to all sin and have no inclination for it. And the nature of
> one who is reborn of the Spirit? According to the particular
> gifts bestowed on each, to grow into that same Spirit into
> which he is born. What is the true nature of a Christian? To
> purify himself in the blood of Christ from all defilement of
> the flesh and of the mind ... and in this condition to eat the
> body of Christ and drink His blood ... What is the true
> nature of those who eat the bread and drink the chalice of
> the Lord? To keep a continual remembrance of the One
> who died and rose again for us ... to live no longer for
> ourselves, but for Him who died and rose again for us.[11]

In the *Asceticon* he takes account of that eschatological aspect of the Christian message so highly prized by the Eustathians, and the peace of soul for which the Greeks yearned. But at the base of the whole structure he puts the twofold aspect of charity – the love of God which leads to a total renunciation of the world, easier of attainment in a solitary life, and the love of one's neighbour which excludes the eremitical life.[12] It is thus the cenobitic life that he extols and he invites all who desire perfection to join a well-organized community rather than multiply small groups 'in the same village.'[13]

This Rule provides for a superior and an assistant in each community and shows us how they are to be appointed.[14] It is not, as in Egypt or in Palestine, a question of a spiritual master drawing disciples to himself, but of a group choosing from its members someone to direct it, who is, as it were, the 'eye' of the body.

> Indeed the right ordering of a religious community demands a superior who is watchful to foresee emergencies, endowed with eloquence, sober, moderate, full of compassion and tenderness, and who, with a truly faultless heart, seeks the faithful carrying out of the commandments of God.[15]

What is important for the Abbot as well as for the disciple who obeys him, is to find out the will of God and to follow it lovingly.

> The Superior, in the sight of God, must look upon himself as the minister of Jesus Christ and the dispenser of the mysteries of God: otherwise, in saying or regulating something contrary to God's will, as made known to us in the Sacred Scriptures, he may be convicted of false witness before God and found guilty of sacrilege ...
>
> And as to what concerns the brethren, he should act towards them as a mother who nourishes and tenderly loves her own children. To make them pleasing to God and for the benefit of all, he should be ready to offer joyfully, not only the trouble and fatigue involved in

preaching the Gospel, but his soul and even his life, according to the word of Our Lord Jesus Christ, who said: 'I leave you a new commandment, that you love one another as I have loved you.' (*John 13.34*) No-one can have a greater love than to give his life for his friends.[16]

He then uses the whole of the *Shorter Rule 114* to explain that what matters is not the dignity of the person who commands, but that the command itself 'should be what is prescribed for us by the law of God or something that conforms to it.' Finally, when there is nothing laid down by rule, one should follow what

> is written: that we should be subject one to another in fear of Jesus Christ, (*Eph. 5. 21*) who said of Himself in the Gospel: 'He who would be great among you, let him be your minister and he who would be first among you, let him be your slave.' (*Matt. 20: 26–27*) He should strip himself of his own will to imitate the divine Saviour who said: 'I came down from Heaven, not to do my will, but to do the will of my father who sent me.'[17]

He states precisely, however, in one of the last of the *Shorter Rules* that one must not put one's own wishes before 'what is commanded by one's superiors', for 'each must stay within the bounds of his vocation.'[18]

It is easy to recognize in all these counsels the teaching that St Benedict was to follow in speaking of obedience, and to see that it came at least partly from the one whom he used to call 'our father, St Basil'.

Other rules of St Basil also touch on the great monastic virtues, for a true gift of oneself to God in love presupposes mastery over one's thoughts,[19] renunciation,[20] silence,[21] self-control,[22] moderation in laughter, words, eating, dress,[23] openness with one's superior, the acceptance of correction with humility, and discretion in dealing with guests.[24]

Another long section is devoted to work and prayer. His spiritual teaching on prayer will be found rather in his commentaries on the Psalms and in his treatise on the Holy Spirit. But here, and in a general way, Basil seems more

concerned with the organization of community prayer than
with the monk's private prayer. He fixes the number of
canonical hours, matins, terce, sext, none, vespers and night
prayers, and disapproves of a desire for contemplation that
would interfere with work and hinder the fulfilment of the
normal duties of community life. For him, private prayer
was that which the monk made during his work. Moreover,
work itself should be chosen in such a way as to 'maintain
the peaceful and tranquil spirit of the religious life'. (*Longer
Rules* 38)

> The way to acquire a spirit of recollection is that, while
> the hands are engaged in labour, one should praise God
> by singing Psalms, aloud or in the heart, thanking God
> for giving us the strength of our hands and our mental
> faculties, asking Him for the success of our work, and
> keeping before us the aim of pleasing Him.[25]

The last of the *Longer Rules* returns to the question of
Superiors, of their duty to correct the brethren, of peace in
the community and, before a conclusion dealing with the
sick, gives some very modern advice to Superiors, namely,
to meet together to study common problems.[26]

There are hundreds of minor regulations, in which practical advice and spiritual counsels are given on almost all
aspects of monastic life. These advice and counsels are
always linked to the teaching of Scripture.

All the ascetical writings of St Basil are so full of balance
and New Testament doctrine that they have been used by
most of the great monastic writers and are still the foundation
of the life of monks in the Eastern churches. They were read
assiduously in the monasteries of the Middle Ages. St Basil
remains for us the man of good sense, filled with the spirit of
the Gospel, whose writings are always worth consulting.

Notes

1   St Basil's letters provide us with many interesting details on his life
     and apostolic work, cf. P.G. XXXII & Y. Courtonne: *Lettres de St
     Basile* and *St Basile et son temps* ed. Budé.

2 cf. Y. Courtonne, *St Basilé et son temps* ch. I & VII
3 ibid. ch. III; *Letter II to St Gregory Nazianzen* (P.G. XXXII).
4 The text of the *Morals* is in P.G. XXXI; English translation in *St Basil, Ascetical Works* (Fathers of the Church, C.U.A. 1962).
5 The *Asceticon* in Rufinus' translation, is in P.L.CIII, 483–564; the *Short and Long Rules* are translated by W.K. Lowther Clarke, *The Ascetic Works of St Basil*, London 1925. The *Long Rules* are translated in *St Basil, Ascetical Works* (Series: *The Fathers of the Church*, Washington 1962).
6 Two texts are particularly interesting from this point of view: his *Letter II to St Gregory Nazianzen* (P.G. XXXII, 223–234) published at the beginning of his conversion and destined for an educated public, develops the Neo-Platonic themes of liberation of the soul from the yoke of the passion, through which the soul is enabled to rediscover the beauty of God in itself. The other is the treatise *To young people on the way of drawing profit from Greek Letters* (P.G. XXXI, 563–590).
7 *Short Rule* 157.
8 In his *Letter* 223. St Basil tells us that he visited Alexandria 'and other places' in Egypt, without mentioning any detail. Moreover his journey took place after St Antony's death; cf. Gribomont: 'St Basile', in *Théologie de la vie Monastique*, ch. V.
9 cf. *Long Rules*: 9: 11–15; *Short Rules*: 1, 98, 114; *Vie Spirituelle*, suppl. XXI, 1952: *Obéissance et Evangile selon St Basile le Grand*, by J. Gribomont. Other scholars think nevertheless, that the organization of the communities was more advanced than said by the author. The passage quoted speaks clearly of a Superior 'who is at the head' of the community. Moreover St Basil wrote several letters concerning the way of life of nuns: *Letter 173 to Theodora; Letter 207 to the clerics of Caesarea*, cf. Y. Courtonne, *St Basile et son temps*, ch. VII.
10 *Long Rules*, 6.
11 *Morals*, Conclusion, P.G. XXXI, 840.
12 *Long Rules*: 1–7.
13 ibid. 35.
14 See also ibid. 45.
15 ibid. 35.
16 *Short Rules*: 98.
17 ibid. 1.
18 ibid. 303.
19 *Long Rules*: 5.
20 ibid. 8.
21 ibid. 13.
22 ibid. 16.
23 ibid. 17–25.
24 ibid. 26–36.
25 ibid. 37. cf. Thomas Merton: *The Climate of Monastic Prayer*, pp. 68–69.
26 *Long Rules*: 54.

CHAPTER VIII

St Gregory Nazianzen and St Gregory of Nyssa

St Gregory Nazianzen

St Gregory, born about A.D. 330, was a friend and fellow-student of St Basil. He accompanied him into the solitude of Annessus, but the austerity of the life and of the surroundings, and perhaps of his friend's leadership, prevailed on him to return home to his father, the elder Gregory, Bishop of Nazianzus. There he was leading a retired life, devoted to prayer and study, when his father, against his own inclinations, ordained him priest. Later on, Basil, who wished to have suffragans to support him in his Councils, consecrated him bishop of a small town. He did not take up residence however, but remained where he was to help his father. He was elected Patriarch of Constantinople, but resigned at the end of two years, disgusted with the opposition of some of the bishops. He returned to Nazianzus and finally retired into solitude where he died about 390.

Gregory had the temperament of a poet, was extremely sensitive – an idealist. He often spoke of the monastic life, but more to praise its aims than to describe its institutions. Among his numerous writings, it is chiefly in his poetical works and in particular in his *Carmina Theologica* that he refers to monastic life.

What is striking about his general attitude towards it is his spirit of proportion, moderation and flexibility. He appreciated the diverse forms of religious life existing in his time, even when obligations of charity made it necessary to live in the very bosom of the family;[1] and the sight of a Stylite on his lofty eminence evoked no censure, though he considered it exaggerated.[2] But this breadth of mind went hand in hand with a desire for authenticity. 'Honour your calling',[3] he flung at the nuns who made a parade of perfection without practising it and a little later he adds:

> You who are betrothed to Christ, offer your all to God. The monk who renounces the world in spirit and holds himself aloof in body, is radiant with beauty.[4]

Better indeed to marry than to enter into dangerous relationships which are a scandal to Christians and a sin.[5]

On the contrary, the function of the monastic state is to shed light, to edify and to guide Christians by putting before them in their most perfect form the virtues they ought to practise – virginity as superior to marriage, detachment in the use of riches[6] and, above all, the love and imitation of Christ.[7] This, his primary duty,[8] the monk exercises through prayer by day and night,[9] detachment from the world, and through 'hymns, prayers, vigils ... self-denial.'[10] It is also a means of redemption for the world, 'Whose faults are covered by the flood of tears',[11] and serve moreover as instruction and light for non-Christians, showing them a way that leads to God.[12]

For Gregory this ideal is realized most fully in the state of virginity. In his childhood he saw in a dream the radiance of its beauty and was strongly attracted to it throughout his life. No subject did he treat with more emphasis[13] and holy fervour, for it is the reflection of the beauty of Christ in man. He often called virgins 'Christophers' (Christ-bearers)[14] that is to say:

> Servants of the cross, despising things of the world, dead to what is earthly, devoted to what is of heaven; lights of the world, mirrors of the wondrous Light. They contemplate God who is theirs and to whom they belong.[15]

Virginity is then the expression of the desire for union with the Absolute, with God, with true reality. This implies a hard struggle after the pattern of Elijah, John the Baptist, Christ Himself.[16] It presupposes poverty[17] and, above all, humility, following the example of Christ who humbled himself even to the death on the Cross.[18]

In all this there is no scorn for the true values of the world; he praises marriage for its dignity which enhances the value of virginity and blames those virgins who condemn the state from which they themselves have sprung.[19] He loves poverty but criticizes the neglect of one's possessions,[20] and values manual labour as a form of apostolate.[21]

After this, one is more inclined to accept his demand that the monk must imitate the angelic life. By this he does not mean an unreal retreat from the world, but an ideal life, wholly directed towards the contemplation of the Trinity in an ever deeper and more constant effort to draw closer to God.[22]

But, as a great lover of the Theotokos, his chosen model was always the Virgin Mary, the true source and radiant manifestation of the ideal of Christian virginity.[23]

St Gregory of Nyssa

St Gregory (335–394), the younger brother of St Basil by at least five years, studied under his elder brother's guidance and thereby acquired an unrivalled knowledge of the philosophies of his time. He undertook a careful research into the principles of Christian faith, basing it on Scripture and on the teachers who had preceded him, in particular the great Alexandrians, Clement and Origen. He uses with perfect mastery the terminology and the concepts of Platonism, Neo-platonism and Stoicism.

Although St Basil asked him to adopt the monastic life, Gregory at first refused, possibly because he could not see how to reconcile it with intellectual research and its apostolic fruit. So, he became a teacher of rhetoric and married. It was then that Basil sought his help in introducing the monastic life to the educated public of Cappadocia. This was the origin of his *Treatise on Virginity*. Soon afterwards in 372, Gregory was consecrated by his brother as Bishop of Nyssa.[24] In this capacity he did his best to support Basil in his struggle against the Arians. After his brother's death in

379, Gregory inherited his labours and strove to continue both the controversial theological writings and the spiritual advice which Basil had given to the monastic communities.

The confidence placed in him by the Emperor Theodosius drew him to Constantinople, which perhaps explains why he wrote little for the monks at this period. Matters changed about 386. Theodosius established himself at Milan and took St Ambrose as his counsellor. This left Gregory free to look after the affairs of his own region. At about the same time, his wife, Theodosia, died. As a widower he was more at liberty to devote himself to an ascetic monastic life; his treatise on virginity had already shown his longing for it. To guide the monks in their spiritual life, he composed *The Life of Moses*, followed by commentaries on the Psalms, the Wisdom books, on the *Song of Songs* as well as an ascetical work *On Perfection*.[25]

The *Hypotyposis*, or *De Instituto Christiano* is an important work. Some specialists attribute it to Gregory, others to Pseudo-Macarius, but it certainly develops Gregory's ideas on monastic life.[26]

After his death, in 394, Gregory's influence made itself felt in the East, chiefly through the popularization of his ideas by Pseudo-Macarius. They form also the link between the Alexandrians and Denis the Pseudo-Areopagite; finally, it was to influence Evagrius and Cassian, and was widely disseminated in the West until the Middle Ages.

The contribution of Gregory of Nyssa to monastic spirituality

The thinking of Gregory of Nyssa was developed throughout his successive writings in a typically Eastern manner, by constantly returning to the same themes, each time at a deeper level. His last works and the *Hypotyposis* were meant for the already well-organized Basilian communities, who wanted an intellectual justification for their life, and a study of monasticism adapted to it.

In his treatise on virginity, Gregory begins by praising this virtue and the saints who practised it. The Virgin Mary, Elijah, John the Baptist, and Miriam the sister of Moses are thus offered in turn as examples. He shows next how one ought to possess all the virtues; actual physical virginity, with its asceticism, is merely the outer shell and the support of an interior virginity, which finds its source and model in the relations between the Persons of the Trinity. In freeing itself from earthly desires the soul is purified and is united with or rather assimilated to Christ in a mystical union which makes it rediscover its links with the Father and the Spirit. Gregory concludes with a criticism of some monastic abuses; the exaggerated austerity of the Eustathians and the illusions of the Messalians who refused to work under the pretext of unbroken prayer.[27]

The *Life of Moses* is an allegorical interpretation of the life of the spiritual teacher of Israel. He becomes the model of monastic life and the symbol of the ascent to God with whom the soul is united in the purification and the mystery of the cloud.[28] The same ideas are developed in his *Homilies on the Song of Songs*[29] and are taken up again more fully in the *Hypotyposis*.

This work, also called as we have said, *The Christian Institute*[30] is addressed explicitly to the Basilian communities 'practising in common the apostolic life', and offers them a small compendium of spirituality. After some introductory sentences he describes the purpose of the book:

> Since you already possess this 'understanding' and have directed your 'love' in a way that accords with the true nature of your souls, you are come together with fervour to imitate the pattern of the apostolic life, by your conduct within your community ... And now you want me to act as your guide on your life's journey and to show you the 'goal' of this way of life and the will of God, together with the road that leads to this 'goal'.[31]

These lines, apparently so simple, take on an unsuspected richness when one notes the technical terms embodying Platonic concepts doubtless well-known to his readers. The 'goal' discussed in the last lines echoes the title of the book which could be translated literally *The Goal According to God*. This idea of a goal to be attained in life is fundamental to Platonism. It is also linked with the 'love' that inclines the soul towards its end.[32]

Gregory adapts these concepts, applying them to Christian monastic life. In the striving towards the goal to be attained, he does not, as Plato does, oppose the nature of the soul against that of the body – spirit against matter – but the state of corruption in which man exists because of sin against the primitive ideal state in which he reflected the will of God. The goal to be attained then is to recover this comformity. This cannot be done except through the understanding of truth, the 'gnosis', which for him as for St Paul (*Heb. 5.14*) is 'the discrimination between good and evil'.

These ideas are expressed in the first lines of the book,[33] but there also, their Platonic context gives them a richer sense. The 'understanding' helps us to discern the true good from that which is only apparent, because it shows us what are true 'realities'. It is then ultimately the knowledge of God, the source of all good, whose image rests in the depths of the soul, 'the receptacle of the Holy Spirit'.[34] It is found more distinctly when the soul is purified from the evil tendencies that corrupt it. But for Gregory, as for the Alexandrians, the source of this knowledge is in the Scriptures.

> Accordingly, I write these first principles of instruction for you, selecting them from among the fruits the Spirit has given me, but often using also many words of Scripture as a proof of what I say and to clarify its meaning. I do this for fear I should seem to renounce the divine gifts God has given me, substituting for them the products of my own mind, or perhaps tracing out an ideal of piety in accordance with the teachings of non-Christian philosophies and, puffed up with vain pride, misusing the Scriptures in my ignorance.[35]

Gregory sees then very clearly the limits of the non-Christian philosophies which he uses so skilfully. They do nothing, as he says elsewhere, but put one on the way to the understanding of Christianity. After defining the goal of monastic life, he explains that faith and baptism are its foundation. One must note in this connection that the spirituality of Gregory of Nyssa is essentially liturgical. The Church possesses the Divine life and communicates it through the sacraments; and man must turn to the Church to receive them.[36] Through them he grows to maturity, but this is the combined work of grace and freedom. The development of this theme of working together, 'synergy', of man offering himself to God to be purified by Him, fills all the middle part of the treatise[37] and was to remain a classic text throughout all the Christian East.

> The Holy Spirit's grace causes the soul to flourish as far as its supreme beauty by cooperating with the efforts of all those who follow him... For the body grows without our help ... the beauty of the soul is renewed by the grace given it by the Holy Spirit and by the zeal of the one who receives it. Its growth depends on her dispositions: the measure in which you strive for love, will be also the measure of the greatness of the soul's development.[38]

St Gregory invites the ascetic to make efforts, so that the action of the Holy Spirit may manifest itself in him. He implies a human effort based on faith and on the power of the Spirit. But, ignoring this point of view, many writers of the next generation were to place human effort before grace. It is from this that Pelagianism took its rise.

The combined work of God and man results in spiritual freedom whereby the soul becomes betrothed to Christ through virginity and in humility unites itself to Him. Man must also strive towards an ever deeper intimacy with Him, without stopping on the way, as St Paul urges in his letter to the Philippians (*Philip. 3.13*), a verse frequently cited.

A second part of the work speaks of community life and takes up the essential points in the teaching of St Basil – the renunciation of one's own will to follow that of Christ, considering oneself as possessing nothing and devoting one's services to the community. Superiors must give an example of this service and train those under them, 'sometimes by chastisement, sometimes by counsel and sometimes by praise.'[39]

Finally, the last section, Gregory's original contribution, concerns prayer, the summit of the ladder of virtue. Gregory resumes here a synthesis of what he had developed in the commentary on the Canticle and on the life of Moses. Like Moses, man sees God 'from behind', in a manner at once luminous and obscure:

> God showed Himself to Moses first through light, then He spoke to him in the cloud; finally when he had become more perfect, Moses contemplated God in darkness. The passing from obscurity to light is the first severance from false and erroneous ideas about God. When the mind has become more attentive to hidden things, it leads the soul through what is visible to the invisible reality and is like a cloud which hides all that is apparent to the senses, accustoming the soul to the contemplation of what is hidden. Finally, the soul that has travelled by these paths to the things of Heaven, leaving all earthly matters behind, as far as is possible for human nature, penetrates into the sanctuary of the knowledge of the divine, surrounded on all sides by a divine darkness.[40]

He comments elsewhere:

> The more the soul, as it advances with an ever deepening and more perfect ardour, reaches an understanding of what the knowledge of reality means, the more it realises that the divine nature is invisible; ... the true knowledge of Him whom it seeks, the true vision of Him, consists in seeing that He is invisible, for He who is sought transcends all knowledge, separated completely by His incomprehensibility as by darkness.[41]

In order to grasp this obscure presence, God develops in the soul new spiritual senses – an idea that Gregory borrows from Origen. He speaks also of a 'sober intoxication', using a term taken from Plotinus; then he forges his own vocabulary, speaking of a 'conscious sleep' the condition of the 'awakening of the soul to God' of 'tranquillity', of 'quietude' and finally of the 'awareness of the divine presence', when the bride of the Canticle

> is surrounded by the divine light in which the bridegroom draws near without revealing Himself ... but gives the soul an assurance of His presence while eluding clear consciousness.[42]

Terms and descriptions are used with a precision till then unequalled, which were to open the way to Christian mystics. But Gregory goes still further; this knowledge is not static; it sweeps the whole man up in an outburst of prayer that carries him ever onward.

> He who applies himself to prayer, taking the Spirit as his guide and support, burns with the love of his Saviour and throbs with desire, never finding satiety in his prayer but always inflamed with the good.[43]

In this continual transport the soul is purified, abandoning itself to the attraction of the divine beauty, and perceives the love of God (*agape*) descending to fill its yearnings (*eros*) to the full. God is not merely a vague infinitude; He is a living spring pouring life into the depths of the soul. He is the 'hidden spring', but

> while in all other wells the water is motionless, in the bride alone it flows to her inmost being, so that she possesses at the same time the depth of the well and the constant flow of the river ... Totally assimilating herself to the supreme Beauty, she imitates the spring in becoming a spring, life in being life, water in becoming water. Living is the word of God, living the soul that receives the word into itself.[44]

But this union is essentially union with Christ; it is with Him that the bride unites herself to enter into God.

> The bride praises the skilful archer who knew so well how to direct his shaft to her ... the archer who is love

(*agape*). That God is love we have learned from Holy
Scripture, He who sends His chosen arrow, His only Son,
to those who are to be saved ... to implant the archer
himself in whoever is pierced by the arrow, as the Lord
has said: 'I and the Father are one and we will come and
make our abode with you' ... O glorious wound and
gentle stroke, through which life penetrates to the inmost
being, opening for itself by the rending of the arrow, a
gate, as it were, and a passage. For no sooner does the
soul feel itself pierced by the arrow of love than its pain is
transformed into nuptial joy.[45]

Thus joined with Christ, all men will be united again in the
New Adam and will be carried into a living union with the
triune God.

When perfect love has driven out fear, then all that are
saved will grow in an ever closer union with the unique
Goodness, and all will be one in the other and one in the
perfect Dove ... Thus encircled by the unity of the Holy
Spirit as with a bond of peace ... all will become a single
body and a single soul ... But better to turn again to the
very words of the divine Gospel: 'That all may be one, as
Thou, Father, in me and I in Thee.' The bond of Unity is
the Holy Spirit.'[46]

The *De Instituto Christiano* ends on this theme. Prayer is
the spiritual joy of the Kingdom of God. It brings the Holy
Spirit to dwell in the soul and is a source of charity in the
community. Both brethren and superiors must make it
possible for those who are drawn to deeper prayer to devote
themselves to it for the good of all.[47]

St Gregory's achievement was to complete the work of
St Basil in giving to monachism a theology and a mysticism
at once deeply Christian and Trinitarian. It complements
the contemplative studies of the Alexandrians who, as they
peer through the obscurity of the divine presence, are
careful to present God as light. In the course of centuries
we have seen the influence of Gregory's work in both East
and West. It assumes an added importance in our day

when contact with the mysticism of Asiatic religions is again drawing the attention of Christians to the mystery of the ineffable God.

Notes

1 P.G. XXXVII, 597, 1470; see J. Plagnieux, *Théologie de la vie monastique*, ch. VI. Most of our quotations come from this article.
2 P.G. loc. cit. 1456.
3 ibid. 908.
4 ibid. 913.
5 P.G. XXXVIII, 88–89. Gregory was chiefly attacking the 'Agapetae', who introduced into their house persons of the opposite sex for 'spiritual espousals'.
6 P.G. XXXVII, 1463–1464; 167–170.
7 ibid. 537; 189 ss.
8 P.G. XXXV, 1063. 'Generis nostri primitias'.
9 P.G. XXXVII, 1454, 30.
10 P.G. XXXV, 1063.
11 ibid. 594.
12 The whole passage tends to prove the superiority of Christian ascetics over the Greek philosophers.
13 For example P.G. XXXVII, 538, 1451. The dream is recounted ibid. 1353 ss.
14 ibid. 538, 1454.
15 ibid. 538.
16 ibid. 1453; 1454, 1455.
17 ibid. 1454, 1463, 1467.
18 P.G. XXXV, 848. Above all St Gregory insists on the humility of the Pastors in the service of their flocks 'forma gregis'.
19 P.G. XXXVII, 542, 547, 551.
20 ibid. 1351.
21 ibid. 783, 19–20.
22 ibid. 523; 526 ss., 591 ss., 636 ss., 644: 662 ss., 1455.
23 See for example ibid. 537, 575.
24 In Cappadocia at this period bishops were allowed to marry. We have seen that it was so in the case of the older Gregory, the father of St Gregory of Nazianzen.
25 Gregory of Nyssa was translated by Scotus Erigena and seems to have excerted great influence on St Bernard and the revival of mysticism in the XIIth century.
26 J. Daniélou *Platonisme et Théologie Mystique* and L. Bouyer *Histoire de la Spiritualité Chrétienne*, Vol. I attribute the *Hypotyposis* to Gregory. Gribomont and Staats consider Pseudo-Macarius as its author.

27 *De Virginitate.* P.G. XLVI. 317–416. Holy Trinity as model of virginity, see ibid. 321, 324.
28 *Life of Moses,* P.G. XLIV, 297–430.
29 *Homilies on the Canticle* P.G. XLIV. See in particular Hom. XI, ibid. 1000, C, D; Hom. VII, 924, A; Hom. XV, 1104, D; 1105. C.
30 The text given in P.G. is very incomplete. W. Jaeger gives the complete text in *Gregori Nysseni Opera,* vol. VIII, *Opera Ascetica,* pp. 40–89.
31 *De Inst. Christ.* W. Jaeger, op. cit. pp. 41, 10–18.
32 See Plato: *The Banquet.*
33 W. Jaeger, op. cit. 40, 1, 6; 41, 3, ss.
34 ibid. 41, 23.
35 ibid. 42, 17; 43, 8.
36 See Daniélou: *Platonisme et Théologie Mystique,* pp. 27 ss.
37 W. Jaeger, op. cit. 43–63.
38 ibid. 46.
39 ibid. 64–69.
40 *XI Hom. on the Cant.* P.G. XLIV, 1000, C–D.
41 *Life of Moses* P.G. XLIV, 376, D-377, A.
42 *XI Hom. on the Cant.* P.G. XLIV, 1001, B.
43 W. Jaeger, op. cit. 78.
44 *IX Hom. on the Cant.* P.G. XLIV, 977, A, D.
45 *IV Hom. on the Cant.* ibid. 852.
46 *XV Hom. on the Cant.* ibid. 1116, C, D.
47 W. Jaeger, op. cit. 82.

CHAPTER IX

St John Chrysostom

His life and works

St John Chrysostom was born at Antioch about A.D. 344.[1]
His father, a general in the army of the Eastern Empire, died
young and John was brought up by his pious mother,
Anthusa. His education took place in the religious atmosphere that surrounded Bishop Meletius and some austere
hermits, such as Julian Sabas, who lived nearby. When John
had completed his studies, at the age of eighteen, he joined a
group of anchorites and spent four years in the desert, at
first under the direction of a master and later in solitude.
On his return to Antioch he became a cleric. As soon as he
was ordained priest in 386 he was put in charge of the
preaching in the cathedral, and at this period delivered
many of those sermons that have made him famous as the
greatest Christian orator, and gained for him the title
Chrysostom or 'golden-mouthed'.

Elected Bishop of Constantinople in 397, he still lived
with monastic austerity, trying by his writings and preaching to raise the faithful to Christian perfection. His life was
harassed by religious and political troubles. In 402 he
welcomed the Origenist monks, driven from Egypt by the
Patriarch Theophilus of Alexandria. Among them was John
Cassian who was always to regard John Chrysostom as his
spiritual master. At this time disagreements with
Theophilus forced St John Chrysostom into exile. He was
soon recalled, but his outspoken criticisms of the licence of
the court involved him in trouble with the Empress Eudoxia
and he was again exiled in 404. He died of fatigue and
wretchedness in 407.

Few of his copious writings deal specifically with monasticism. His homilies were aimed at drawing his people to
God. He talks about various subjects, but always keeps the
monastic ideal in the background, as a term of comparison.
His ideas on monastic life occur in short passages[2] throughout his work and must be considered as a whole, because
rhetorical emphasis sometimes leads him to use unqualified
terms that in isolation misrepresent his thought.

In dealing with spiritual matters, St John Chrysostom
chooses what will profit lay people and, from this stand-
point, has little to say of monastic institutions. In his time
monachism was already thriving and existed in various
forms. But it must also be remembered that all who consecrated themselves to God in a life of voluntary poverty and
celibacy – people whom we would now call 'religious' –
were then indiscriminately regarded as 'monks'. The
comparison between this ideal of perfection and that which
was more suited to the laity led St John Chrysostom to
speak with precision on what constitutes the religious life,
the different vocations it admits and their place in the
Christian community. He thus shows himself as a precursor
of the spirituality of the laity and the declarations of
Vatican II on religious and monastic life.

The essence of the religious according to St John Chrysostom

St John Chrysostom asks ordinary Christians to imitate
many aspects of the religious life. He recommends meditation on Scripture to all, for

> Knowledge of Scripture strengthens the mind, purifies the
> conscience, roots out the enslaving passions, sows the
> seed of virtue, produces unworldly thoughts, saves the
> soul from being overwhelmed by the unexpected vicissi-
> tudes of life, releases man from the snares of the devil and
> makes him dwell close to Heaven itself.[3]

Scripture also sustains the Christian in prayer, which must
be constant. Some ascetics are completely absorbed in it:

I should like you to be thus absorbed, if not always, at least often, if not often, at least sometimes, at least in the morning and evening, but if you cannot raise your hands in prayer, raise your free souls as far as is possible.[4]

Elsewhere he recommends prayer in church, before meals and during work; preferably this should consist in the chanting of psalms.[5]

When he speaks of monks, he constantly returns to the virtues of voluntary poverty, virginity and compunction, (this last being the realization by the conscience of our state of sinfulness), the necessity for practising asceticism, and prayer for constancy in the struggle. All these virtues are equally necessary for all Christians according to their state in life. The fact that religious follow the evangelical counsels indicates no difference in the goal but only in the means of attaining the same ideal of Christian perfection.

It is a monstrous mistake to think that monks must lead a perfect life while the rest need not bother. It is the duty of lay people as well as of monks to reach the same summit of perfection.[6]

This common summit is love in a total surrender of self to God, with a faith of which Abraham is the model.[7]

Let us love with this love, to which nothing else is comparable. Let us love thus for the sake of the present or . for the future; better still for the sake of love itself. In this way we will escape punishment and attain the kingdom of heaven. Besides, both the realm of darkness and the kingdom of heaven amount to nothing compared with the happiness of being loved by Christ and of loving Him.[8]

Christian perfection thus consists in being drawn by love to the Master who loves us: 'once begun it grows and never ceases.'[9] Every Christian strives to attain it according to his particular vocation. It is natural for a religious to put himself in those privileged conditions that will facilitate his spiritual progress. By practising the evangelical counsels, he frees himself from the obstacles that hamper the Christian in ordinary life.

So the apostles left all to follow Christ and because they left all, they were able to follow Him more easily.[10]
What is there more certain or more noble than to have one care only, that of pleasing God.[11]

It is not then a question of counting up acts of virtue but an interior attitude of a deliberate approach to God. St John Chrysostom uses many comparisons to illustrate his point, for instance, the soldier, the wrestler, the runner,

who runs with all his strength and pays no heed to obstacles even if he encounters them a thousand times; but, completely engrossed on his course, passes everything with ease, and hastens on to the appointed goal.[12]

The dangers on this road are sadness and slackness. Against these difficulties St John Chrysostom repeats the advice of St Antony,[13] not to dwell on the past but to make repeated fresh beginnings.

The only way not to lose one's head is not to look at the height that has been reached but, on the contrary, to examine what we still have to ascend and to go there with decision.[14]

He goes on to praise

the soul that drives itself towards the desired goal, disdains the earth and, raising itself above all visible things, hastens to the Master.[15]

This is the true meaning of poverty and virginity, practised for God. The religious life constitutes a privileged path towards perfect love but, within itself, has room for different ways, all fulfilling essential functions in the Christian community.

The role of different religious vocations within the Christian community

Imitating the disciples of Antony, the ascetics of Antioch and Constantinople left the towns to seek a solitude favourable to prayer.[16] But, like Basil, Chrysostom recognized the need for chosen souls, to exercise the most difficult apostolic tasks in the very heart of the community. In fact he complained that concern for souls was in peril,

> for some do not care about virtue, and the others who do care, leave the ranks.[17]

He tried accordingly to attract to the town religious men and women competent to take charge of hospitals,[18] teaching,[19] care of the poor, and even of an apostolate among the laity, which would resemble the role now played by secular institutes.[20] Finally he ordained certain ascetics because their work demanded it and so that they could inspire the general body of the clergy with their zeal.[21] Still others he called to the hardest missionary tasks in pagan territories, Persia, Armenia, Phoenicia.[22]

But Chrysostom had no intention of depopulating the solitudes, and held in esteem those who passed their lives in prayer and penance.[23] It was a question of vocation and he would not allow one to be praised to the detriment of the other. It is not necessary

> that after examining the lives of the solitaries, we denigrate those who serve the churches, whose lives have much in common with the former but in secret. Let us be careful not to despise them because they enter houses, go to the market place, preside at assemblies (for prayer) ... The paths of virtue are many; as varied as pearls ... they vie with flowers in the variety of their radiance or can be compared with the diffusion of the sun's splendour. Such are the saints; some practise their virtues by themselves; others in the midst of the Church.[24]

These vocations to a life of Christian perfection have a definite part to play in the Church. All Christians are called to
perfection but they must have examples to draw them.
Those who practise virtue to the highest degree, virginity
instead of chastity, poverty instead of giving alms, etc. show
other Christians that perfection can be attained according
to one's state in life.

> Are you afraid of such moderate commands (of Christ),
> when you see others advance beyond this goal? We only
> ask you to give alms; others have given up everything. We
> merely ask you to live chastely with your wife; others
> have given up marriage completely.[25]

At a deeper level, the religious life is a sign and witness of
the Incarnation which reconciles man with God. God has
always given signs by which men may recognize Him: the
marvels of the Old Testament, the miracles of Christ and, at
the present time, the martyrdom and the 'philosophy of
monks'.[26] Like Adam before his fall, they are masters over
their instincts.[27] By virginity, by their efforts to remain in
the presence of God, and by the service they give to their
fellow-men, they share in the life of the angels.[28] Virginity,
poverty and charity are signs of the renewal brought by
Christ, they are a pledge of Redemption and show all men
that they are 'citizens of heaven' making a short stay on
earth.[29]

> Look what a service these strangers render you, these
> travellers, these citizens of the desert, or rather citizens of
> heaven. We are strangers with regard to heaven, citizens
> of the earth; with them it is the other way about.[30]

Over and above the duties common to all who consecrate
themselves to God, each vocation has a special role to play.
It is obvious that those who work in the bosom of the
community

> acting as a leaven for the rest, lead many to imitate their
> own fervour.[31]

But those who dwell in solitude, either in the desert or hidden in the towns, must keep in their hearts concern for the salvation of their brothers, and Chrysostom is indignant against the self-centred who flee, seeking solitude only for their own interests:

> Would it not be better for you to become less fervent yourself than to remain on the heights, looking with indifference on your brothers who perish.[32]

True monks, on the contrary have a deep concern for the Church and never stop praying for her:

> In all kinds of ways they are crucified to the world. As far as they can, they assist those in charge of the Church, strengthening them by their prayers, by their union with them, by their charity.[33] ... they are lights that illumine the whole earth. They are ramparts that protect cities. This is their reason for settling in solitudes – to teach us to despise the futile agitation of the towns.[34]

A light does not hide itself; hence the monks have a duty to offer hospitality:

> Monasteries are light-houses that shine from above to give light to those who come to them from afar; safe in the harbour, they invite all to share their tranquillity, not permitting those who see them to suffer shipwreck or to remain in darkness.[35]

The bishop also zealously encouraged the faithful to make a few days' retreat in one of the monasteries, even offering to lead them there himself.[36]

St John Chrysostom had the gift to discern the role played by different religious vocations in the Church. Virginity and poverty, animated by prayer, meditation on Scripture and a fervent love for Christ and for souls, are practised with the aim of fulfilling the hardest tasks in the Church – the apostolate of the towns, distant missions, and the service of praise and supplication as a support for pastors and faithful.

Notes

1 Most of the information given in this chapter comes from the article of J.M. Leroux: 'Monachisme et Communauté Chrétienne', in *Théologie de la vie monastique* ch. VII.
2 These texts have been collected in the following works: L. Meyer: *St Jean Chrysostome, maître de perfection chrétienne*; E. Boularond: *La venue de l'homme à la foi d'après St Jean Chrysostome*; Dom Ivo der Maur: *Mönchtum und Glaubensverkundigung in den Schriften des Hl. Johannes Chrysostomus.*
3 *V Hom. De studio praesentium* I, P.G. LXIII, 485.
4 *In Hebr. Hom.* 22, 3 P.G. LXIII, 208, A.
5 *In Matt.* 2, 5. P.G. LVII, 30; *In Eph.* 21, 2. P.G. LXII, 151.
6 *Adv. opp. vit. mon.* 3, 14, P.G. XLVII, 372.
7 *In Rom. Hom.* 9, 1. P.G. LX, 467, B.
8 *In Act. Apost. Hom.* 6, 3. P.G. LX, 60.
9 ibid. *Hom.* 8, 2. P.G. LX, 72.
10 *In Matt. Hom.* 64, 1. P.G. LVIII. 610.
11 *Ad Theod. Laps.* II, 5. P.G. XLVII, 315.
12 *In Gen. Hom.* 28, 6. P.G. LIII, 259, c.
13 He was an assiduous reader of the life of St Antony and made it known to all about him. cf. *In Matt. Hom.* 8, 5. P.G. LVII, 89, B.
14 *In Psalm.* 119, 1. P.G. LV, 339.
15 *In illud: scimus quoniam.* 3. P.G. LI, 169, A.
16 It is this aspect of personal salvation that John Chrysostom seems to have had in mind when he himself left for the desert. cf. L. Meyer, op. cit. pp. 29, 233, ss.
17 *In Eph.* I, *ad cor. Hom.* 6, 4. P.G. LXI, 53–54.
18 *Pallad. Dial.* 5. P.G. XLVII, 20, c.
19 *In Matt. Hom.* 59, 7. P.G. LVIII, 584, B.
20 *Adv. opp, vit. mon.* III, 12. P.G. XLVII, 368, 370.
21 *Pallad. Dial.* 15, 47, 51. *De Sacerdotio* VI, 8. P.G. XLVIII, 684.
22 *Let. LIV ad Geront.* P.G. LII. 683; *Let.* 221 ibid. 753; *Let.* 53, ibid. 637; *Let.* 55, ibid. 639.
23 *In Gen. Hom.* 42, 5. P.G. LIV, 392; *De Sacred.* III, 15. P.G. XLVIII, 652.
24 *In I Trin. Hom.* 14, 6. P.G. LXII, 576.
25 *In Matt. Hom.* 39, 4. P.G. LVII, 438.
26 *In I Cor. Hom.* 6, 3. P.G. LXI, 52.
27 *In Gen. Hom.* 18, 4. P.G. LIII, 153; ibid. *Hom.* 12, 5. P.G. ibid. 104, B. *In Heb. Hom.* 3, 2. P.G. LXIII, 30.
28 The same theme is found in the *Life of St Antony.*
29 *In Matt.* 8, 4. P.G. LVII, 87; *In Psalm.* 119, 2. P.G. LIV, 332, A.
30 *In Matt. Hom.* 55, 6. P.G. LVIII, 423, 424.

31 *In Gen. Hom.* 43, 1. P.G. LIV, 396.
32 *In I Cor.* 6, 4. P.G. LXV, 54.
33 *Contra Anom.* VI. P.G. XLVIII, 496, D.
34 *In Matt. Hom.* 72, 4. P.G. LVIII, 672.
35 *In I Tim. Hom.* 14, 3. P.G. LXII, 574.
36 *In Matt. Hom.* 72, 3. P.G. LVIII. 670.

CHAPTER X

Pseudo-Macarius and Evagrius Ponticus

PSEUDO-MACARIUS

The problem of Pseudo-Macarius

We have seen that Macarius the Egyptian, the organizer of the monastic colony at Scete, was most certainly a great spiritual father. A whole monastic literature has been attributed to him, only a fraction of which, however, is definitely authentic. But there is a collection of writings (fifty *Homilies* and a *Great Letter*), which have a marked unity of style and thought. The author is an unknown monk, a disciple of St Gregory of Nyssa, but drawing inspiration also from the wisdom of the Egyptian deserts and in particular from Macarius, from whom these works take their name.

Only in recent years, scientific research[1] on the texts makes it possible to distinguish which of the recognized works of Gregory really belong to the Pseudo-Macarius. The same research work permits also to establish their interdependence.

In the first place, Pseudo-Macarius has a distinctive style, simple, imaginative and fervent, recalling the literature of the desert and making its ideas accessible to all. Moreover, writing after Gregory, he profits from the development of institutional monachism, and in speaking of it, is able to use expressions familiar to all towards the end of the fourth century, instead of the often vague terms of his predecessor. But the originality of Pseudo-Macarius is primarily in

choosing certain themes from St Gregory, isolating them
and giving them a new emphasis.

Prayer – the principal work of the monk

The *Great Letter* is for the most part a popularization of
De Instituto Christiano, which it follows step by step. But
it draws special inferences from the remarks which
Gregory makes, in accordance with St Paul, enjoining
humility and charity within the community. He applies this
teaching to the different occupations of the monks, some
having charge of material tasks while others are at prayer.
Macarius refuses to choose between prayer and manual
work, exalting one at the expense of the other.[2]
Commenting on the episode of Martha and Mary, he sees
the preference given to prayer, but maintains that the text
teaches equally the necessity and the dignity of manual toil.
He follows this up, however, by the passage in Acts where
the Apostles judge prayer to be more important than
serving at tables.[3]

To understand the thought of Macarius, one must remember that for him, as no doubt for St Basil, St Gregory and all
their monastic circle, prayer impregnates work and is
inseparable from it. The experience of the Desert Fathers led
them even to consider work as an aid to prayer. They
compared it to an anchor that settles the thoughts.[4] It was
not, therefore, a choice between prayer and manual toil, but
an insistence on prayer and on the necessity for giving it first
place in the monastic life, according to each individual vocation. Encouragement must be given to those who wished to
devote more time to solitary prayer, while remembering that
a man should work at prayer and not avoid giving needful
service to the community.

The *Homilies* likewise insist on prayer as the monk's
essential activity, permeating all other occupations.
Constancy in prayer had already been stressed in the
Apopthegmata attributed to Macarius the Egyptian, who at
the same time encouraged the monk to struggle against
temptations and

to say with each breath:
'Our Saviour, Jesus Christ, have pity on me,
I bless thee, Lord Jesus, help me'.[5]

The Pseudo-Macarius also insists on keeping guard over the heart as a condition of prayer:

The Apostle says, 'I wish men to pray without anger or evil thoughts'. Now, according to the Gospel, it is from the heart that evil thoughts arise. Look at yourself, then, in prayer; examine your heart and your mind, have the intention of sending a sincere prayer to God, and be careful to notice whether your prayer is pure, whether your mind is intent on the Lord like the labourer on his work, the husband on his wife.[6]

This effort is made to develop in the soul that attention of the Lord wherein

the soul puts everything aside for prayer and the love of Christ, fixing all its attention on Him.[7]

These expressions were to be taken up later and developed by the Hesychast current of Greek monachism, seeking in silence and solitude the quietude (*hesychia*) needful for continuous prayer. The Pseudo-Macarius did not go so far, yet considered prayer the essential activity of the monk.

The sum total of all good actions, the highest of all our works, is perseverance in prayer, through which we can each day acquire all the virtues by asking God for them. Prayer wins for those who are judged worthy, communion with the holiness of God, with the energy of the Holy Spirit, and union of feeling with the mind of the Lord in ineffable love. The man who daily makes the effort to persevere in prayer is consumed by the spiritual love of a divine *élan* and burning desire for God, and receives the grace of sanctifying perfection.[8]

Sin and grace

The effort of attention to God and of prayer presupposes for the Pseudo-Macarius, as for Gregory of Nyssa, a progressive purification of the soul, a constant struggle between good and evil, between the tendency to sin and grace of God, which draws men to Him. At the time they were writing, this theme had been developed by the heretic Messalians to the point of leading them to profess the co-existence in every person of a principle of good and a principle of evil. Macarius, however, did not consider this co-habitation as normal. For him, grace never ceased to fight against sin and the faithful must strive for simplicity of heart to be accepted by Christ.

> The soul has many parts and great depth, and once sin has entered, it spreads through all these parts and the pastures of the heart. But, when man begins to seek for grace, it comes and fills perhaps two parts. Then the inexperienced man, encouraged by grace, thinks that by its coming it has spread itself to all the compartments of the soul and sin has been eradicated. In fact, the greatest part is still dominated by sin and only one part by grace. He is deceived and is not aware of it ... studying and examining the import of these words, you will of necessity become even more wise in the Lord, growing in simplicity of heart through His grace and the power of His truth so well that ... freed from all distraction and deceit of the enemy, you may be found upright and unconquered on the day of Our Lord Jesus.[9]

Mysticism of light

A last aspect taken by the Pseudo-Macarius from the work of Gregory of Nyssa, is contact with God as the source of light. His failure to mention the element of darkness in God's approach constitutes a regression in thought, but from the warmth of expression used, we feel that Macarius is here revealing something of his own spiritual experience. All striving towards God culminates in the simplicity and purity of soul that reflects God in the same way as a mirror without blemish.

> If you have become the throne of God, and the heavenly Wagoner has rested upon you, and your whole soul has become a spiritual eye and wholly light; if you are fed with the food of the Holy Spirit, if you have drunk the water of life, and are clothed in the garments of ineffable light; if your inward being has enjoyed the fulness of all these experiences, behold, you truly live the life of eternity.[10]

The works of Pseudo-Macarius had a great influence on the whole of Eastern monachism. Popularizing some of the deeper intuitions of Gregory of Nyssa, with a lyricism and simplicity that made them accessible to all, he still attracts by the profound aspiration that permeates his work – the search for God, union with Christ, contemplation of the glory of the Lord in the joy of the Holy Spirit.

EVAGRIUS PONTICUS

His life and works

Evagrius (345–399) was born in the small town of Ibora on the Black Sea. He was the son of a *chorepiscopus* and took orders himself while still young. St Basil ordained him as reader, and in 379, shortly after the death of Basil, he was ordained deacon by St Gregory Nazianzen, who made him archdeacon in his own see of Constantinople. He was thus able to take an active part in the second ecumenical council of Constantinople, where he made a spirited defence of the faith of Nicea against the Arians.

His success made him worldly and he neglected his spiritual life. Passionately loved by the wife of a high dignitary of the court, he was on the point of giving way to temptation when, in a dream, he saw himself arrested and imprisoned. There and then, he vowed to leave the capital and look after his soul. He left for Jerusalem, where he was welcomed at the monastery directed by Melania, who helped him to reform his life. After another crisis when he became seriously ill, he decided to leave for Egypt. He became a monk at Nitria, then went to Scete to put himself under the direction of Macarius the Egyptian. He lived there in humility and obedience, renowned for his gentleness and tranquillity. His death took place on the Feast of the Epiphany 399. He asked to be carried to the church to take part in the sacred mysteries, received Holy Communion and fell asleep in peace.

No doubt the Lord wished to spare him the troubles which came during that same year to the group of monks called Origenists to which he belonged. The Patriarch Theophilus of Alexandria drove them from Egypt and condemned them. Palladius and Cassian were among the exiles who took refuge in Constantinople.

This condemnation of the Origenists brought about the destruction of the Greek writings of Evagrius, which were thus only very imperfectly known until the recent discovery of the complete texts preserved in Syrian, Arabic or Armenian versions.

His work divides into two categories; first speculative, theological writings, in which Evagrius drives to their extreme conclusions certain erroneous ideas of Origen, thus causing their condemnation. The most important of these works are the *Gnostic Chapters* (*Kephalia gnostica*) and the *Epistle to Melania*. His other works touch on asceticism and mysticism. Here he is much more orthodox and, cultured Greek as he was, gives us a synthesis of the spiritual and psychological experience of the Desert Fathers. It is the teaching of these works that we shall consider.

The most important are the *Praktikos*, with its introduction, the *Letter to Anatolus*, a treatise on prayer,[11] and the *Centuries on Prayer*.[12]

Evagrius' treatment of mysticism

Evagrius was a Greek, trained in the ideas of Neo-Platonism, and a disciple of Origen; from this milieu, he borrowed, with slight modification, the notions on the world and on man that govern his entire thought. The Universe was first wholly spiritual; matter is not necessarily evil in itself, but it was created because of sin, and it is spiritualized by making reparation. Temptations assail us through our bodily passions, which disturb and paralyse the soul, and it is impossible for man to aspire to union with God without having first purified his heart.[13]

Stages in spiritual progress

Gregory of Nyssa and Pseudo-Macarius had begun to discern a progression and different stages in the spiritual life. Evagrius was the first to define the successive steps in the soul's advance towards union with God. Doubtless he did no more than codify the spiritual and psychological experience of the Desert Fathers, which we can surmise, but only in a fragmentary manner, from the *Apopthegmata*. Fr. J. E. Bamberger, in his notes to his edition of the *Praktikos* shows its close affinities to the discoveries of modern psychology.

For Evagrius, the first stage in the spiritual journey is what he calls the 'active' or 'practical' life, in which the soul struggles to master various irregular tendencies or affections, to develop virtues and to carry out the commandments: 'This is the spiritual method which has for its goal the purification of that part of the soul whence the passions arise'.[14] This stage ends in *apatheia*, a state of peace that opens the way to charity and contemplation.

Gnosis, that is, 'knowledge' or contemplation is the second stage, which is divided into two phases – contemplation of the created, and 'Theology' or 'contemplation of the Trinity', which we shall explain later. After having taken this general survey, we must now examine more fully the chief elements of the spiritual progress.

Virtues, vices and commandments

The Desert Fathers had specialized in the study of 'thoughts'; they had observed how thoughts come and go and studied their relationships with each other. On the basis of these observations, Evagrius was likewise able to distinguish eight fundamental vices, that we now call the seven capital sins; gluttony, lust, avarice, melancholy, anger, sloth (*acedia*) or distaste for spiritual effort,[15] vainglory and pride. Each of these vices invokes and gives strength to the others, but they are paralleled by an even stronger chain of corresponding virtues:

> The fear of the Lord strengthens faith, and continence, in its turn, reinforces this fear; patience and hope establish these virtues in firmness and also give birth to *apatheia* (peace of soul). This has a child called charity which holds the gateway to deep knowledge of the created universe. Finally, to this knowledge succeeds 'Theology' and the 'supreme beatitude'.[16]

The test of these virtues is the fulfilling of the 'commandments'. Here we come again upon the theme treated by St Basil and St Gregory of Nyssa, that of the will of God on which man must model his conduct. Evagrius considers it under a slightly different aspect, maintaining that the fulfilment of the commandments is one of the great means of purifying the heart. This idea was to be taken up later by Cassian and St Benedict.

Apatheia

Thus the fruit of purification, through obedience to the commandments, is *apatheia*, a word already employed by Clement to describe the peace of the soul that has mastered its passions (*pathe*). It can be described as the deepest repose of the soul, by a tranquillity that manifests itself even in dreams, and by an ability to judge objectively, without yielding to the pressure of personal feeling. It is preserved by the fear of the Lord, nourished by humility and sorrow for sin. But it is never acquired to perfection. One must always be on guard to protect it, because it is exposed to the constant assaults of the devil. It blossoms finally only in charity and contemplation.

The strength of the commandments is not sufficient to purify the passions of the soul completely, if contemplation does not then help by engrossing the spirit.[17]

Contemplation

Evagrius repeatedly asserts that for him contemplation or knowledge (*gnosis*) is rooted in charity.

Charity is the highest state of a reasoning soul; in this state it is impossible to love anything in the world more than the contemplation of God.[18]

But he distinguishes two principal stages, first 'natural contemplation', by which, in considering the 'essence' of things, the soul recognizes the presence of God, in the Scriptures, in nature, in symbols. If a man's heart is pure, he draws from this contemplation a knowledge of the attributes of God.

The contemplation of corporal and incorporal beings is the book of God, in which the pure spirit inscribes itself by means of contemplation. In this book also are written the principles that concern Providence and judgement, a book through which one knows that God is creator, wisdom, providence and judge; creator by what has passed from nothingness to existence, wisdom by the hidden meanings of these things, providence by the aids given to guide us in the path of virtue and contemplation, finally, judged by the various forms given to intelligent beings, the diversity of worlds and the changes wrought by the centuries.[19]

In the highest stage of contemplation, the soul reaches simplicity of thought; it rests tranquilly in deep peace and sees itself as the place where the presence of God is reflected as in a mirror. It is as if a radiant light in the soul transforms it and 'carves into it the place of God.'[20]

When the spirit, putting off the old man, reveals the man

born of grace, it sees its own state at the moment of prayer, resembling the colour of sapphire or the sky, what Scripture calls the place of God, seen by our fore-fathers on the mount of Sinai.[21]

These words bring us back to the words of Gregory of Nyssa on contemplation 'in the light and the darkness of Sinai'. Like him, Evagrius has experienced the infinity of the mystery of God, at once present in the heart of man and yet beyond all form and concept. But though Evagrius calls this state 'contemplation of the Trinity', he does not seem to have penetrated into the mystery of it as Gregory had done.

Such as it is, however, his description of the stages of contemplation is particularly interesting in our day, when we are confronted by the mystics of Asiatic religions, who often describe their experiences in similar terms: 'vision of the essence (*tattva*) of things', 'God present in the depths of the soul', the experience of union with Him, the ineffability of the mystery of God. This seems to be the point that unites the monachism of all religions: the search for union with the Absolute, a quest in common which could serve as a point of departure for a better mutual understanding.

But, true as are his intuitions into spiritual life, one cannot unfortunately clear Evagrius from all trace of error. The discovery of the authentic texts of his theological works show that the charges brought against him were well-founded. His value for monastic life rests in his collect-ing into a coherent whole the experience of the Desert Fathers, and his complete surrender of himself to the search for God, encouraging others towards that same goal to which he devoted his life:

Make haste to transform yourself to the likeness of the divine model.[22]

Notes

1 This work has been carried out chiefly by H. Dorries de Gottingen and by W. Jaeger who published the *Great Letter* in an appendix to his volume *Two Rediscovered Works*. Fr. Bouyer gives some details in *Histoire de la Spiritualité Chrétienne*, Vol. 1. ch. XV, which we

also use in this chapter. The quotations from Macarius are taken from it.

2 W. Jaeger. *Two Rediscovered Works,* Appendix, *Macari Epistula Magna,* p. 281 et seq.

3 ibid. p. 288. 9. Act. 6, 2.

4 Cassian *Inst.* book 2. ch. 14.

5 Bouyer, op. cit. p. 452. cf. Amélineau. *Annales du Musée Guimet,* t. XXV (1894), p. 161 and J. Gouillard. *Petite philocaliede la Prière du coeur* (1953)

6 XVth Homily XIII P.G. t; XXXIV 584 C.

7 VIth Hom. I. P.G. XXXIV 517 C; XXXIIIrd Hom. I.P.G. XXXIV 741 C.

8 XLth Hom. II P.G. XXXIV. 764 B.

9 Lth Hom. IV. P.G. XXXIV, D. 821 A.

10 Ist Hom. XII. P.G. XXXIV, 461 D.

11 *The Praktikos* has been edited by Guillaumont in *Sources Chrétiennes.* See Irénée Hausherr *Le traité d'oraison d'Evagre le Pontique,* R.A.M. t. LXV (1935), Bouyer, op. cit. pp. 456–472, from whom we borrow most of the quotations and especially *Praktikos: Cistercian Studies* No. 4, with a commentary by Fr. J. E. Bamberger, which makes reference to more recent studies.

12 The *Centuries* are collections of a hundred sentences on a subject. Apparently without any logical link, they nevertheless comprise in general a quite coherent train of thought. It seems that Evagrius was the creator of this literary form.

13 Hausherr, op. cit. p. 82.

14 *Praktikos* 50.

15 *Acedia,* or the noonday devil, seems to be a special temptation for the monk who grows weary and discouraged by the dryness of the spiritual struggle. Evagrius has given a famous description of this stage; *A Anatole sur les 8 pensées* VII. p. 6, XL, 1273 B.C. Cassian also deals with the same subject.

16 *Letter to Anatolus.* Bamberger, *Praktikos,* p. 14.

17 *Praktikos,* 50–51.

18 The *Century* 86. Fd. Frankenberg, p. 123.

19 *Selecta in Psalmos.* ps. 138, v. 16, P.G. XII, 1661 C (a work of Evagrius for a long time attributed to Origen).

20 *Praktikos* I, 71.

21 idem.

22 idem.

CHAPTER XI

St Jerome and St Augustine

St Jerome

His life (345–420)

St Jerome was born at Sridonium near Aquileia. He went to Rome to study and conceived a passion for classical literature. After baptism he embraced a life of asceticism, at first at Aquileia where, with his friend Rufinus, he combined asceticism with intellectual activity. After some time he left for the East so that he could study monastic life at its source. He passed three or four years in the desert of Chalcis, near Antioch, and there devoted himself entirely to the study of the Bible. This followed a dream in which Christ is supposed to have said: 'You are not a Christian but a Ciceronian'. Ordained priest at Antioch, he travelled to Constantinople (about 379), whither he was attracted by St Gregory and, in 382, went on to Rome, where Pope Damasus engaged him as secretary and charged him with the revision of the Latin text of the Vulgate. At the same time, Jerome introduced a group of ladies of the Roman aristocracy to the study of the Bible and to asceticism. They later settled near him in Bethlehem (385), after the death of Pope Damasus. He remained in close contact with the convents of these ladies and was the superior of a monastery of monks; he stayed there until his death in 420.

Jerome was not a profound thinker but a brilliant writer, a good translator and a Biblical scholar. His passionate temperament led him into disagreements with some of his friends and in particular with Rufinus. He achieved self-control only through a strict asceticism of which study formed a part. His monastic teachings are contained chiefly in his letters and in some of his Scripture commentaries. He also wrote several lives of the Desert Fathers and translated the Rule of St Pachomius.

Themes of monastic spirituality

His principal source of inspiration was Scripture but he also drew much from Origen. Although during his quarrel with Rufinus he had tried to deny his partiality towards the Origenist school of thought, he none the less continued to be profoundly influenced by this great genius. He borrowed from him, in particular, the themes of the Logos-Word of God, considered as nourishment for the soul, the comparison between virginity and martyrdom, the necessity for a vigorous and persevering search for God, and finally the idea that, if it is good to follow the example of the saints, especially of St John the Baptist, modelling one's life upon theirs is insufficient, it is Christ that we must imitate above all. He cites as an example Paula, one of his Patrician ladies, who, with her daughter Eustochium, had founded the convent at Bethlehem.

> She followed the poor Lord,
> becoming poor, even in spirit;
> she gave back to Him what she had received,
> making herself poor for His sake.[1]

Jerome was also the singer of solitude. For him the word 'monk' meant someone alone, in contrast to the people of the town.

> Happy life, disregarding men, seeking angels, leaving the towns and finding Christ in solitude.[2]

Jesus himself retired to the desert to pray during the night. In solitude it is easier to find Him and to see His glory as the disciples did on Mount Thabor.[3]

Prayer and the Liturgy are 'the service of God'.[4] Monks
do on earth what the angels do in heaven, for they also
intercede for the Church. Monks and virgins are the intimate friends of God; the people of the world are like the
servants working in the fields; if they need to ask something
from the master, they approach those who are in daily
contact with Him.[5]

In the face of the then current heresy demanding a second
baptism, Jerome presents monastic profession as a
baptismal renewal that washes sin away as martyrdom
does.[6] This martyrdom is gained not merely by continence[7]
but also by voluntary poverty and the praise of God.[8]

Charity is one of the specific duties of monastic life. It is
shown by helping one another in the community, but it is
also necessary in dealing with guests. Love for Christ gives
the guest-house an important place in the monastery.[9]
There was a continuous flow of pilgrims to Bethlehem, and
the hospitality given them there in the name of Christ to
whom it had been refused had a profound meaning and far-
reaching effect in spreading the teaching of the Gospel,
inviting others everywhere to practise it.

Finally, St Jerome dealt with the question of the function
of monastic life in the Church. Just as the clergy fill the role
of Christ working for the salvation of men, so the monastic
life represents Christ praying to His Father in silence. This
contemplative praise is a bond between the Church militant
and the praise given in heaven. The example of ascetic
monasticism acts also as a stimulant in the Church, and
penance unites monks with the martyrs in their intercession
for her.[10]

Because of the widespread diffusion of his writings,
Jerome helped considerably to make known to the monks
of the West important aspects that linked them with
Oriental monasticism. Paradoxically, it was his contemporary, the African St Augustine, Bishop of Hippo, who was
to give to the spirituality and monachism of Europe many
of the traits that still characterize it.

ST AUGUSTINE

His life (354–430)

St Augustine was born at Thagaste in North Africa in 354, of a pagan father and a Christian mother, St Monica. After pursuing literary studies at Carthage and then at Rome, he taught Rhetoric at Milan. During his youth, he had abandoned the Christian faith for Manicheism and had formed an illicit union with a woman who had borne him a son, Adeodatus. At Milan, under the combined influence of his mother and the bishop, St Ambrose, he recovered his Christian faith and, at the same time, discovered Neo-Platonism, which filled him with enthusiasm and was to provide him with the terminology and intellectual background of his first writings. At the same period, he read the life of St Antony by St Athanasius and this influenced him greatly. In fact, his decision to be baptised was closely linked with that of taking up the ascetic life. A first attempt, at Cassiciacum near Milan, with some friends, did not last long. But he soon returned to Africa and organized a monastery for laymen in his own home at Thagaste. When he became a priest of the Hippo diocese, he founded a second monastery, still with laymen, on church lands. A few years later, now Bishop of Hippo, he asked the clergy he lived with to lead a cenobitic life and continued to live as monk himself until his death in 430.

The Augustinian writings on monastic life are made up of three principal texts: the *Ordo Monasterii*, written around 395 by Alypius (successor of Augustine as head of the Thagaste monastery) which has a feminine version; the *Praeceptum*, written a little later by Augustine, for the monastery of men at Hippo; later, a feminine version was made, the *Regularis Informatio*. The *Objurgatio* is a letter of Augustine to nuns in the same period. These treatises were associated and combined in the letters 210 and 211, and called *The Rule of Saint Augustine*. To these texts should be added Augustine's sermons to monks, 355 and 356, his treatises *De Opere Monachorum*, about the work of monks, and *De Virginitate*. There are also many allusions to monasticism in his other works, particularly in his commentaries on the Psalms.

The monachism of St Augustine

The ideal of monastic life is, without doubt, based on the text of Acts which moved St Antony to decide to leave the world and consecrate himself to God:

> The multitude of believers had but one heart and one soul: neither did anyone say that aught of the things which he possessed was his own; but all things were common unto them ... Neither was there anyone needy among them. For as many as were owners of lands or houses, sold them and brought the price of the things they sold, and laid it down before the feet of the apostles. And distribution was made to everyone, according as he had need. (*Acts 4: 32–35*)

This text has resounded through the world like a prophetic summons, calling monks as a trumpet calls men to battle.

> Hearing it, brothers who wanted to live together, arose. This verse was their trumpet. It has resounded throughout the earth, and those who had been divided were united. The call of God, the call of the Holy Spirit, the prophetic call.[11]

St Augustine's rule can be divided into two parts, one setting out the principles of monastic life, the other demonstrating their practical application. It is this text of Acts that wholly inspires the first part. At the beginning of the Rule he comments on it:

> This is what we recommend you to observe in your monastery: first of all – since this is the reason for your coming together – that you live in one mind in the house and have one soul and one heart directed towards God. There should be no talk of personal possessions; on the contrary, all should be held in common, and to each

should be given according to his need ... Live in unity of heart and soul and each honour God in his neighbour, for you have become His temples.[12]

The Holy Trinity is the foundation and model of this unity in peace. It is brought about through the Holy Spirit who is Love. It is He who united the apostles at Pentecost and who now draws the hearts of the faithful to Christ to unite them in Him. Perfect unity will only be achieved in eternity, following the triumphant Christ, but Christ is also truly present in the Church. Monastic life is the expression of the soul of the Church raising itself to the peace and unity of the Celestial City.

> Men are many but faith makes them one.
> Men number many thousands; through love, they become one. They love God in the fire of charity and, out of a multitude, they attain the beauty of oneness.[13]

The Eucharist nourishes the union of all in the Church and is the expression of this unity, affirmed by the faithful in the Amen of the Communion:

> To that which you are you reply Amen,
> and in that reply you subscribe to it.
> Remember that bread is not made with one grain
> but from many ... and so it is with the wine.[14]

On earth, however, this unity is always precarious; it must be cherished and developed, little by little, to expand in eternity:

> We must love unity and eternity because, being one, we desire to be united to our God and Lord.[15]

From the example of Acts we see also that unity is practised by renunciation of the possession of material goods. It unites us to God by making room for Him in the heart:

> Abstain then, brothers, from all private ownership, or at

least from attachment to it if you cannot give up the possession itself.
It is thus that you make room for God.[16]

Elsewhere he uses a different image. The man who practises voluntary poverty:

Walks with a lighter step on the road that leads to the land where God and true riches are found.[17]

The monastic ideal does not differ from that of other Christians. It is only distinguished on the practical level by a greater generosity, using more radical means to attain its end. But, following the example of the early Christians, who brought their goods to the apostles to be distributed among the poor, monks must put at the service of the faithful the spiritual goods they acquire,[18] in order to lead them all to the peace of Christ.

This solidarity of all Christians is particularly emphasized by Augustine on the occasion of his struggle against the Donatists, who maintained that sanctity was reserved for a few pure souls separated from the mass:

All run in the stadium, says St Paul, but only one receives the prize and the others retire defeated. But it is not so for us. All who run, provided that they continue to the end, receive it and the one who arrives first waits for the last to be crowned with him. For this struggle is the work of charity and not of greed. All who run share a mutual love and it is this love that is their course.[19]

Another controversy – this time with the British monk, Pelagius – led the Bishop of Hippo to define the respective roles played by human effort and grace in this race towards God, sustained by His love. Pelagius had at first done no more than reinforce the terms used by the Greek fathers, for instance, the *synergy* of St Gregory of Nyssa, expressing the joint action of God and man in the progress towards sanctity. But he went on to maintain that, if a man reached the required degree of asceticism, he could, by his own power, attain perfect self-mastery (*apatheia*), and freedom from sin. Augustine, on the contrary, taught that man, impaired by original sin, certainly keeps his free will but, without divine grace, cannot achieve success in the unremitting struggle he must make. Without God's help, he is unable to seek his good effectively.

These statements seemed new-fangled and alarmed many monks, especially those of the south of Gaul, among them Cassian, who feared that one could draw from them the conclusion that effort was useless and that it was enough to wait for grace. These objections led Augustine to state clearly that the first inclination towards God is an effect of grace, but this demands the co-operation of man which makes it possible. Indeed, the love that is in us is a participation in the love of Christ, who will himself draw us into the love in the heart of the Trinity.[20]

But St Augustine was not content to define the part played by grace in man's progress to God; he has himself described the different stages of union with God with a penetration and warmth which have made him one of the greatest Christian mystics.[21] In several of his works he touches on the subject, but his commentary on Psalm 41 gives a clear and complete exposition of the soul's advance towards union with God.[22] 'As the hart panteth after the fountains of water ...'

First of all the soul feels a desire at once vague and intense for a reality that is not clearly known, but which draws it towards contemplation; and when it surrenders to this desire, supernatural truths appear under a new light. At the same time, the extermination of sin and liberation from the passions are seen as necessary conditions for approaching God.

This thirst for God makes us yearn to reach his very self, although in faith. Man cannot find Him in creatures nor in himself; he must look further for a truth and a reality not subject to change or abatement. In explaining the Psalm, Augustine is then led to state that the virtues of the saints, by their example, help the soul to reach the threshold of God's dwelling place. This, he says elsewhere, is the very depth of the soul itself.

After these preliminaries he comes to the mystic experience itself. He compares it with the experience of someone who, having for a moment heard the music of the celestial banquet, is captivated by it and, forgetting all earthly sounds, hastens towards 'the stream of living water', towards the interior sweetness of God, towards 'something of the unchangeable infinitude', perceived as in a flash of light. But soon the soul falls back reluctantly into its habitual state, only retaining in the heart an intense desire to review the experience.

The whole of the commentary on Psalm 41 is magnificent, but unfortunately too long to quote here. An echo of the same experience, however, appears in the *Confessions*. After having little by little penetrated the created world and reached the vision of absolute Reality, of the Unchangeable, he says:

> Then indeed I came to have a sight of thy invisible things ... but I could not fix my gaze upon them. For my weakness being beaten back, I was restored to my wonted objects; and I carried along with me no more than a loving memory of those others, and, as it were, a longing for the odour of those things whereof as yet I was not able to eat.[23]

This consideration of the stages of union with God and its effects on the soul opened the way, in the West, to the study of mystical phenomena that developed in the Middle Ages with St Gregory the Great and St Bernard and then with the Franciscan school, to find its full fruition in the mystics of the sixteenth century, especially in St Teresa and St John of the Cross.

Another idea introduced by St Augustine has had effects that have lasted till our own day. Commenting on the Gospel story of Martha and Mary, and above all on the passage in Genesis concerning the two wives of Jacob,[24] he gives the name 'active' to the life that is concerned with moral and human activities, and 'contemplative' to that spent seeking eternal truth. The former can be practised in this life only, the other is fully developed only in eternity but begins in this life. Taken up and defined a little more exactly by St Gregory the Great, these terms were used to describe as active, the life occupied with good works for Christ, and as contemplative, that which is given up to prayer. Here we have an entirely new conception of these words, for until then they had been used to differentiate the various stages or aspects of the spiritual life. The active life was the struggle against sin; it led as its natural consequence to contemplation, that is to say, the intuition of the divine given by grace, and union with God through love. St Augustine, on the contrary, saw the two kinds of life as opposed to one another. To the active life, simply concerned with leading a good moral life in the world he preferred the attitude of Mary who had chosen the better part and recommended it to the faithful in a prayer that St Thomas takes as a definition of the contemplative life.[25]

> Let them choose the better part, giving themselves up to the word of God, yearning for the sweetness of His teaching, and let them make the object of their contemplation the knowledge that leads to salvation.[26]

For people who must, as a duty, occupy themselves with worldly business, he advises a mixed life, where the leisure of contemplation succeeds action. In the *Confessions* he describes how he himself strove to practise it. Speaking of his intimate union with God, he says:

> This I do often; it is my delight, and as soon as I can free myself from my duties, I return to this pleasure. And sometimes you admit me to an intimate and rare experience of marvellous sweetness.[27]

But Augustine did not consider that this intimate experience of God was reserved for trained souls. He himself, as Gregory the Great did later, preached the contemplative life to the mass of the faithful. Although he believed that only a few reached the heights, the way was open to all simple and sincere souls:

If we are faithful, we have already reached the way of faith. If we do not abandon it, we shall most surely arrive, not only to an understanding of things incorporeal and unchangeable, which cannot be grasped in this life, but even to the heights of contemplation that the Apostle calls 'face to face.' Indeed, some of the most lowly, who walk with perseverance in the way of faith attain this most holy state of contemplation, while others who are endowed by nature with the ability to comprehend the invisible, the unchangeable and the incorporeal, cannot reach this sanctuary of peace, although their minds are already touched, as at a distance by the rays of its light; for they refuse to follow the way that leads to the above of such happiness, that is to say Christ crucified, because this seems foolishness to them.[28]

But, though the joy of contemplation may be open to all, Augustine recognizes that hermits are in the best conditions to foster it:

They enjoy a close relationship with God, to whom they cling with a pure spirit, and are rewarded by the contemplation of His beauty which can be perceived only by the spirit of those who are holy.[29]

It is infinitely regrettable that this doctrine of the different states of life should have become rigid in the eighteenth and nineteenth centuries to the point of reserving contemplation for an elite and confining all others within the narrow limits of discursive meditation. It was one of the benefits of Vatican II to recall that every Christian and above all every priest and religious must have in his life at least a small share in the life of contemplation.[30]

At all events Augustine wished monks and nuns to observe these times of silence in their free moments, when the soul could continue the dialogue with God begun during the Office or simply rest in His presence.

If the brothers sometimes, when they are free, wish to

pray in the oratory, outside the regular hours, they must not be hindered by those who may have taken the liberty of working there.[31]

The remaining prescriptions of the Rule give brief guidelines to help in the practice of detachment of the heart, through poverty and, above all, through charity, for this remains the dominant note throughout. Care of the weak, fraternal charity and obedience, motivated by love, are thus recommended to the brethren and to the superior, who must himself both observe and impose discipline:

> Though both are necessary, let him wish to be loved by you rather than feared, remembering always that it is to God that he must render an account of your souls ...
>
> God gives you all these precepts that you may observe them with love, like religious enraptured by spiritual beauty, who breathe out by the goodness of their lives the sweet perfume of Christ, not as slaves under the law but as free men under grace.[32]

St Benedict was to adopt these ideas in his Rule, but before that, they began to influence the rules of the many monasteries that began to multiply in the West. These we must now examine, beginning with the work of Cassian. A contemporary and sometimes adversary of Augustine, he is the spokesman of the Oriental monastic tradition in Europe.

Notes

1 *Ep.* 108, cited by P. Antin in *Théologie de la Vie Monastique,* p. 193. The quotations from St Jerome are taken from this article.
2 *In Mc.,* Corpus Christianorum (C.C.) LXXVIII, ibid. p. 195.
3 *Ep.* 3, 4.
4 *In Ps.* 119. C.C. LXXVIII, p. 257.
5 *In Ps.* 139, C.C. LXXVIII, p. 284.
6 *In Ps. 115,* C.C. LXXVIII, p. 245; *Ep.* 39, 3, 4; *Ep.* 130, 7, 14.
7 *Théologie de la Vie Monastique,* p. 198.
8 *In Ez.* 40, 42. P.L. XXV 391, C. *In Ps.* 81, C.C. LXXVIII, p. 90. *Ep.* 120, 11, 9; *Hom. in Luc,* 16, 19, 31, C.C. LXXVIII, p. 516.
9 *In Ps.* 133, C.C. LXXVIII. p. 289; *Ep.* 125, 14, 2 and 15, 2.

10 See J.P. O'Connell. *The Eschatology of St Jerome*. Mundelein, Illinois 1953.
11 *In Ps.* 132, 2. P.L. XXXVII, 1729.
12 *Rule of St. Augustine* Ch. 1.
13 *De symb. sermo ad cat.* II 4, P.L. XL, 629. quoted in *Théologie de la Vie Monastique* ch. X. *St Augustine* by M. Veheijen, p. 207. We have followed this article for the commentary on the text of Acts and have taken most of the quotations from it.
14. *Serm.* 272. 1. P.L. XXVIII, 1246.
15 *In Ps.* 4, 10. P.L. XXXVI, 83.
16 *In Ps.* 131, 6. P.L. XXXVII, 1718.
17 *De Civ. Dei,* V. 18. P.L. XLI, 164.
18 *Contra Faustum,* V. 9. P.L. XLII. 226. *De op. Mon.* XVI, 17 P.L. XL 562 et seq.
19 *In Ps.* 39, ed. Vives, t. XII. P. 276.
20 See Bouyer, *Histoire de la Spiritualité Chrétienne.* Vol I, p. 572.
21 The mysticism of St Augustine has been studied by Dom. C. Butler in *Western Monachism,* from which we have taken what follows.
22 *In Ps.* 41. P.L. XXXVI. 464 ss. See also *Confessions* VII, 16–23, IX, 23–25, X, 65; *De Quantitate Animae* 74–76; *Genesis ad lit.* XII; *Ep.* 147, *De Videndo Deo; C. Faustum* XXII 52–58; *De Civ. Dei* XIX 1, 9, 18; *Serm.* 103. 104.
23 *Confessions* VII, 23 (11) (Butler, op. cit. p. 48)
24 Martha and Mary *De Trin.* I, 20 Rachel and Lia, *C. Faustum* 52–58. See also St Peter and St John, *Tract. in Jo* LXXIV 5.
25 St. Thomas. *Summa* 2.2. Quest. 181. art. 3.
26 *Serm.* 104, 2. (Butler, op. cit. p. 166)
27 *Confessions* X. 65. (ibid. p. 165)
28 *Ep.* CXX, 4. (ibid. p. 166)
29 *De Mor. Eccles.* I, 31, 66 (ibid. p. 167)
30 Vat. II, p. c. 5; p. o. 12.
31 *Rule of St Augustine.* ch. II.
32 ibid. ch. VI.

CHAPTER VII

Cassian

His life (360–432) and works

Although Cassian supplies many autobiographical details in his Works,[1] uncertainty hovers over his youth. From his own testimony we know that his family was well-to-do and deeply Christian, but specialists are doubtful as to whether they belonged to Gaul or to the shores of the Black Sea, the latter hypothesis seeming the better founded. Whatever may be the place where he first saw light, his birth must have taken place about 360. After a sound classical education, while still very young, he felt the call to the monastic life and with a companion, a little older than himself, Germanus, he set off for Palestine. The two friends were received into the monastery at Bethlehem, 'not far from the cave where Our Lord deigned to be born of a virgin', doubtless before St Jerome settled there. But the reputation of the monks of Egypt and their occasional meetings with a few of them, induced the two young men to ask permission to visit the ascetics of that country. This was given on the condition that they promised a speedy return. But the attraction was so powerful that they waited seven years before returning to Bethlehem for a short visit to furnish themselves with the necessary permission to remain in Egypt. In particular they visited the hermits of Lower Egypt and settled at Scete, making visits also to the Cells where Evagrius lived. But about 399, the persecution launched by the Patriarch, Theophilus of Antioch, forced Cassian, Germanus and many other monks accused of Origenism to flee to Constantinople where they were received by St John Chrysostom. He divined the worth of the newcomers and attached them to his clergy. Germanus became a priest and Cassian a deacon.

The teaching and oratorical genius of Chrysostom made a lively impression on Cassian who vowed complete allegiance to the saint and, towards the end of his life, loved to say that he learned from him all that he knew. He probably meant in the matter of doctrine. Unfortunately, shortly afterwards, John Chrysostom was driven into exile, but the clergy and the faithful of the town charged Germanus and Cassian to go to Rome with a letter of appeal to Pope Innocent I.

Cassian was in Rome in the Spring of 405; his stay in the Eternal City lasted about ten years and while there he formed a bond of friendship with the future Pope, St Leo. It was probably here that Germanus died and Cassian was ordained priest. Soon after 415 Cassian travelled to Marseilles where he founded two monasteries, one for monks and the other for nuns. He spent the rest of his life, till his death about 432, governing these monasteries and working for the development of monastic life in Provence. The bishops, founders and superiors of the region begged him to commit to writing the treasures of monastic experience he had amassed on his journeys in the East. This resulted in two books, the *Institutes*, describing the life of the Egyptian monasteries, and the *Conferences*, explaining the spiritual doctrine that animated them.

Towards the end of his life a trial beset him. With many other abbots and bishops of Provence, he had been disturbed by the inflexibility of certain propositions of St Augustine on grace, which, by making everything depend on it, seemed to constitute a danger to monastic fervour and an encouragement to relaxation. But Cassian lacked the metaphysical acuteness of the Bishop of Hippo, and his masters, Origen, Athanasius and Chrysostom, were vague on the subject. Moreover, he thought it his duty to maintain, though wrongly, that a man could at least sometimes initiate a good action and could then draw grace from his initial goodwill (Conf. 13, ch. 8). This error is hardly apparent except in *Conference 13* and does not affect the rest of his teaching.

Let us now look more closely at the *Conferences* and *Institutes*. The *Institutes* consist of two sections. In the first (books 1–4), the author speaks of the monastic habit and its significance; then of the office and the monk's way of life. In conclusion he gives the discourse pronounced by the Abbot Pinufius at a clothing, which forms a kind of summary of monastic teaching.

The second part (books 5–12), without mentioning the source, takes up the teaching of Evagrius on the eight capital sins. Its aim is to point out the efforts necessary at the beginning of monastic life, to purify oneself from the passions. This is what Evagrius calls the 'practical' or 'active' life; its aim is to prepare the soul for the higher gifts of contemplation.

The *Conferences* divide into three books. The first, consisting of ten Conferences, describes the essential factors of the monastic life, the aim of a monk's life, discretion, the three renunciations, then the struggle against sin, spiritual trials and prayer. Books two and three, each composed of seven Conferences, give further treatment on various points of the spiritual and monastic ideal, both for cenobites and hermits.

Cassian's monastic teaching

Cassian's aim was to transmit to the monks of Gaul the monastic tradition of the East, particularly that of Egypt, in a way that would be useful to them. One must not, therefore, expect a detailed commentary on the monks in the valley of the Nile, but an intelligent selection, emphasizing the ideas the author judged essential for those he was addressing. Among the numerous monasteries he had visited, Cassian chose those of Egypt as models. He justified his choice on two occasions in an effort to prove that the Egyptian traditions go back to the Apostles themselves.[2] The historical arguments which he thought he had found may not stand up to criticism, but they do return to the true notion that the monastic life tries to be an 'apostolic life', continuing the life of Jesus with the twelve and of the first Christian communities in Jerusalem as described in Acts.[3] Monks isolate themselves from the mass of the faithful only that they may live this life in full, to show the Church its true countenance, its essential sanctity, and to increase it to the fullest dimension. The Egyptian monasteries are outstanding because the generosity of their asceticism, their balanced teaching and the spiritual experience bring them closest to the apostolic model, and give their institutions a particular educative value.

But another idea also underlies Cassian's argument. The monastic life is a difficult one and cannot be improvised. To practise it well one must enter a tradition, let oneself be formed by experienced elders, and comply with the observances that have made them saints:

> In the whole of Egypt and the Thebaid ... monasteries are not ruled according to the whim of each ascetic, but were founded to continue by order of succession and the traditions of the ancients ... Again no one is chosen to rule over a congregation of brothers unless he, who is to be put at the head, has learned in obedience what he must demand from his subordinates, and unless he has acquired through the training of his own elders, what he is going to pass on to the young.[4]

Without this training, false kinds of monks arise, like the Sarabites who:

> Show themselves just as eager to dress up with the name of monk as they are little disposed to imitate a monk's life. They do not care about monastic discipline, nor to subject themselves to the authority of their elders, nor to learn from them how to overcome self-will; for them no regular training, no rule dictated by a wise discretion.[5]

False monks fall away from monastic life and from the Gospel. If, on the other hand, a man wishes to be a perfect follower of Christ, a threefold renunciation is required:

> The first is material; this makes us scorn all the riches and goods of the world. By the second we bridle our past way of living, our sins, our passions of mind and body. The third consists in withdrawing the mind from things

present and visible, to fix them entirely on the life to come and to desire only the invisible.[6]

Cassian develops this idea in other Conferences, showing that the first stage comprises not only poverty but also celibacy and non-violence. Poverty includes manual toil to earn one's bread and to give alms; virginity comprehends the renunciation of family and the privileges of social status, and non-violence, understood in its broadest sense, includes obedience, at least non-resistance to the will of another.[7]

But above all Cassian wishes to make clear, and this surely constitutes his essential message, that all these exterior sacrifices do not make the monk. They are nothing without a renunciation of the heart. By asceticism the monk frees himself from the Law by surpassing it, for he does more than is prescribed for laymen, but all is intended to lead him to the liberty of a heart detached from sin and orientated towards the acquisition of virtue, whose crown is charity.

> Make haste then, if you thirst to attain true perfection, to renounce the heart as you have renounced the body, family, country, the riches and pleasures of the world, and never turn back to desire what you have renounced ... We must banish the vices with haste and holy eagerness and dispel the abundance of sin acquired by our inner man ... If we do not know how to detach ourselves from them and suppress them while we are still in this life, they will not cease to accompany us after death. Just as virtues acquired here below, especially charity from which all spring, clothe with splendid beauty, even after death, the man who loves them, so do vices darken the soul.[8]

This second renunciation is essential in the thought of Cassian. The passage quoted goes back to the part of the *Institutes* where the practices mentioned in the first section are spoken of as a support in the struggle against the sins described in the second; and this idea of the 'practical life'

or 'apostolic life' leading to charity that triumphs over all
sin, occurs many times in the *Conferences*. In other respects
Cassian does no more here than follow the traditional
teaching of Antony, Gregory of Nyssa and Evagrius. Like
them, he considers monastic life not merely as a series of
austere observances, but primarily as an attempt to purify
the heart from vice, and as an impulse towards virtue and a
charity culminating in contemplation. This is no more than
a prefiguring of life in eternity, to prepare for which is the
aim of the third renunciation. Cassian states this aim as
early as in the first *Conference* attributed to Abbot Moses:

Moses: Purity of heart then must be the goal of all
                    our actions and the object of all our desires.
                    And so it is right to refer secondary things,
                    such as fasts, vigils, retreats, and meditations
                    on Scripture to our principal goal, that is to
                    say, purity of heart, which is charity ... This
                    must be the chief target of our efforts, the
                    unchangeable purpose and constant passion
                    of our hearts – to cling always to God and
                    things divine ...

Germanus: We should like to know how, and in what
                    measure, the spirit can unite itself to God
                    who is invisible and incomprehensible.

Moses: To cling to God ceaselessly and remain
                    inseparably united to Him in the way you
                    say, yes, it is impossible for man in the weak-
                    ness of the flesh. But we must know whither
                    we are constantly to direct our spirit,
                    towards what object we must continually
                    turn our soul's gaze.[9]

The role of the elders, ministers of the Tradition, is to guide
the monk by way of his threefold renunciation, in order to
lead him to God and unbroken prayer. The chief obstacle to
master in the soul is self-will. One must ceaselessly bring it
into accord with God's will by keeping the commandments

and striving after virtue.[10] The whole art of the spiritual master lies in the discretion that removes snares of excess of all kinds and

> discerns all a man's thoughts and acts, examines them, and in the light of this, sees what he must do.[11]

Anchorites as well as cenobites need this training, but the superiority usually accorded to the former derives from the fact that they aim directly at 'union with Christ, the mind detached from all that is earthly', in the secret of their aloneness with God and the total gift of a love that does not count the cost.[12] But cenobitism has its own merits. First of all that of training, because, for Cassian, even hermits ought to be formed in a community. The cenobitic life also allows a greater degree of renunciation, absence of material cares, which favours union with God, obedience, but, above all, fraternal charity, which through daily sacrifices bestows peace and love.[13]

Moved by charity, Christian monasticism is an expression of the Church as the loving spouse of Christ.[14] Sustained by the words of the psalms 'the soul reaches this purity of prayer which is no longer expressed by words, but springs up like fire, inexpressible delight, insatiable impetuosity. Leaving behind her senses, and all visible things, the soul offers herself to God in sighs and groans beyond words.[15]

In the history of monachism, Cassian is one of the most important links between East and West. He himself drew his themes from the Cappadocian Fathers, from the Masters of the Egyptian desert and from St John Chrysostom. In diverse ways he, in his turn, was to transmit to St Benedict and the West their conception of obedience and moderation, their teaching on humility and prayer and, finally, their conception of the divine office.

Notes

1 For the life of Cassian, see Dom E. Pichery, *Introduction to the Conferences. Sources Chrétiennes.* No. 42. O. Chadwick, *John Cassian*, Cambridge 1968.

2 *Inst.* 2, 5: VII. 17–18; *Conference* XVIII, 5–8: XXI, 30; See A. de Vogüé; *Monachisme et Eglise dans la pensee de Cassien, Theologie de la vie monastique,* ch. XI, an article that we have followed for this part of the account. It has been translated into English in *Monastic Studies* No. 3. 1965.
3 *Acts* 4: 32–34.
4 *Inst.* II, 3, 1 and 3.
5 *Conf.* XVIII, 6
6 *Conf.* III, 6.
7 Poverty to include work, *Conf.* XXIV, 12. Almsgiving, *Conf.* XX, 8; XVIII, Virginity, detachment from family, *Conf.* XXIV, 10–12. Non-violence in the form of patience, gentleness, obedience to one's neighbour, *Conf.* XVI, 15–20.
8 *Conf.* III, 7–8.
9 *Conf.* I, 7, 8, 12, 13. Conf. XXIV, 6.
10 *Conf.* XVIII, 7–8.
11 *Conf.* II, 2. The whole of this conference is devoted to discretion.
12 *Conf.* XVIII, 6. XIX, 8.
13 *Conf.* XIX, 6–8. Inst. IV. *Conf.* XXIV, 26. *Conf.* XVI, especially 3, 6, 14, 16, 18.
14 See A. de Vogüé, loc. cit. pp. 233–234.
15 *Conf.* X, 11.

CHAPTER XIII

The Western Rules

HISTORY OF THE RULES

Cassian wrote his monastic works at the request of the Abbots of Provence. The age preceding the barbarian invasions saw an extraordinary development of monachism in Gaul. St Martin contributed much to this advance. Sulpicius Severus tells us that two thousand monks assisted at his burial.[1] But his very success shows that his work was part of a general development. In a very short time, numbers of monasteries were established, and from the fifth to the the seventh century, there was a flowering of monastic rules, fortunately collected for posterity by St Benedict of Aniane in his *Codex Regularum* at the end of the eighth century.[2] If we add a few missing fragments, known from other sources, to the twenty-five that he copied out, we have thirty rules altogether.[3]

The history of the Rules is complex, because there is a close literary dependence between them, each author drawing freely on the writings of his predecessors as was the custom at the time.

At the beginning, we find three principal texts with little dependence on each other; the *Rule of St Basil*, translated by Rufinus, that of Pachomius, translated by Jerome, and the Monastic Texts of St Augustine. What might be called the first generation of Western Rules was composed by Cassian, who drew his inspiration from Pachomius and from Basil, and following that, a quite independent rule, the *Rule of the Four Fathers* (Serapion, Paphnutius and the two Macariuses), which seems to have no more than slender links with the three first authors and with Cassian. One of the most interesting features of this Rule is its opening, which deals with the community, then of the superior as an agent of unity in the community and lastly of the obedience that brings it about.

This Rule, as well as the writings of Cassian and Augustine, were to have a direct succession that is easy to trace. The influence of Basil and Pachomius,[4] on the contrary, is more diffuse and can be traced in many different monastic systems.

The *Rule of the Four Fathers* was written by the founders of Lerins at the beginning of the fifth century. The *Second Rule of the Fathers*, also composed at Lerins, depends on the previous one and on Augustine. This small work had a subsequent influence out of proportion to its size. At the beginning of the sixth century the *Rule of Macarius* appeared; the author was probably Porcarius, Abbot of Lerins. This rule depends on Jerome and Cyprian and reproduces half of the *Second Rule*. A few years later the *Regula Orientalis* appeared, also a Lerinian work, depending on Pachomius and the *Second Rule*. In 535, the *Third Rule of the Fathers* was written at the Council of Clermont; it makes use of *Macarius* and of several Gallic councils. In the last quarter of the sixth century, the *Regula Tarnatensis* was drawn up, depending on Pachomius and on the *Second Rule*.

The Augustinian trend had begun to develop, a few years previously, with the appearance in the first third of the sixth century of the *Rule for Nuns*, by Caesarius of Arles, followed by his *Rule for Monks*, which summarizes the former and adds a few passages.

The successor of Caesarius in the See of Arles, Aurelian, in about 548, wrote a rule for monks combining the two Rules of his predecessors and making another for nuns.

Belonging probably to the first quarter of the sixth century and almost contemporary with Caesarius of Arles, is the *Rule of the Master*, a work that derives from Cassian. The Master draws his inspiration also from Basil. In about 530, the Neapolitan, Eugippius, wrote a Cento *Rule*, a compilation from Augustine and the Master, Cassian, Basil, Pachomius and the *Rule of the Four Fathers*. St Benedict wrote his Rule between 530 and 560, drawing on the

Master and Cassian, but remoulding in an original synthesis elements from all his predecessors, Pachomius, Basil, the *Historia Monachorum*, the two *Rules of the Fathers*, and, above all, Augustine, to which must be added the *Apophthegmata of the Fathers*, translated at Rome in Benedict's life-time.

Although our enquiry stops with the time of Benedict, we must point out that the formulation of new rules continued after him. In Italy, in the second half of the sixth century, we have the *Regula Pauli et Stephani*, which makes prudent use of Augustine, Basil and Pachomius; in Spain in the seventh century, rules compiled by St Isidore of Seville and later by St Fructuosus of Braga, while at the same period, Irish monachism appeared with the Rules of St Columbanus which, in their application, were very soon to be associated with the Rule of St Benedict whose influence was spread by the Columbanian movement. It is echoed in the Rules for Nuns of Donatus and of Waldebert (*Regula Cujusdam Patris*) which combine them in different ways, Donatus adding the rule of Caesarius of Arles.[5]

SPIRITUAL TEACHING OF THE RULES

The main trends and their evolution

Though differing in literary form and in length, these rules nevertheless form a compact ensemble, because of their common purpose, that of regulating cenobitic life, and because they are based on doctrinal principles drawn from the same texts of Scripture, interpreted in a similar way. We have seen also their close literary interdependence.

Looking at them as a whole, however, one can distinguish successive waves of influence which give to every age its own distinct character. The influence of Augustine, almost non-existent in the *Rule of the Master*, manifests itself in Caesarius of Arles; and Benedict, too, owes much to him, if not in extent at least in depth. This influence had its repercussions in Spain with Isidore of Seville. It grew weaker then, to be replaced by the influence of Cassian on Fructuosus and still more on Columbanus. The Benedictine Rule then comes to the fore, at first in association with other rules, then reigning alone from the time of St Benedict of Aniane.

Caesarius of Arles and his contemporary, the Master, imposed a certain number of new regulations which were preserved after them and made their Rules a kind of dividing line in the history of monastic legislation. These additions were matters of definition rather than real innovations. They deal first with the formalities of admission. A written agreement was required before monastic profession and the renouncement of property. Clothing took place at the end of the probationary year and not at the beginning as Cassian had stated.

In the same way, these rules give minute descriptions concerning the Office. It varied according to the season and this variability affected the daily time-table as well as the times of fasting. Finally, small cells for one, two or three monks were replaced by a common dormitory, either for the whole community or for groups if the community was a large one.

These changes were due, at least in part, to a growth in learning among the monks and also to their increase in numbers and importance in society. This brought about a modification in the respective roles of Abbot and Prior. The latter became more important sometimes at the expense of the Abbot. Increased social obligations and the complexity of the material organization of the monastery, often obliged the superior to be absent and to appoint a substitute for the direction of the community. In the Rule of St Benedict, we have a reflection of the tensions that could be produced by the duality of direction thus brought about.

This situation contributed also to changes in the literary field. In the first place, to precision of terminology; the superior, formerly called 'Father of the Monastery' or 'the one who presides' (*is qui praest*) or prior (*praepositus*), is named 'Abbot', a name already used by Cassian; from the time of Caesarius and the *Rule of the Master*, the name 'prior' being reserved for his assistant.

The foregoing remarks concerned all the Rules, whatever religious family they belong to. We must now notice a few characteristics peculiar to the Gallic tradition.

First of all, we mark the importance given to sacred reading (*Lectio Divina*), now just as obligatory and sometimes as long as the Office itself. This custom came probably from Jerusalem, through Egeria's description of her pilgrimage. It was emphasized by the British monk Pelagius, who unfortunately turned to heresy. He wished the first hours of the day, when one is most disposed for it, to be devoted to reading and meditation on Scripture.

Another feature of Gallic monachism was the extreme length of the Office, together with the diversity of its composition. Certain Rules go so far as to impose twelve Psalms for each of the 'little hours' of the day! Was this emphasis on the Office perhaps due to the fact that monasteries were sometimes the foundations of princes, who provided for the monks' needs, on condition that 'they prayed for them'?[6]

The composition of the Office varied with each Rule, as did the manner of saying it. The important thing was that the monk should remain with God, should pray the whole day. *Lectio Divina,* Office and asceticism were considered as means to this end, the methods and proportions of their use being adapted by each superior to the needs of his community. This makes it easier to understand the freedom with which Saint Benedict made changes in the Divine Office he had received from the Master, a freedom he meant to transmit to his successors.

Till now we have been considering Western Rules as a whole; each has given indications that have enabled us to follow the evolution of the monastic world of these regions at the beginning of its history. They were not necessarily all of the same value. The difference in their lengths alone suggests this. Some are confined to a few pages, indeed, to a single one in the *Second Rule of the Fathers*, and the majority stretch to a third or a fourth of the Rule of Saint Benedict. Some Rules, however, have played a decisive role in history. We have already spoken briefly of the *Rule of the Four Fathers*. Let us look a little more closely, first, at the Rule of Caesarius of Arles and then at that of the Master. The first is a good example of short rules and the second, being the longest rule ever written, is it own recommendation.

Rule of Caesarius of Arles

Caesarius,[7] formerly a monk of Lerins, became Abbot of a monastery on the outskirts of Arles, then Bishop of the same town, in 502. He died in 542. His monastic works are first, a letter of exhortation (*Vereor*) and a Rule, for the nuns of Saint John's monastery, built near his Cathedral. This community was headed by his sister, Caesaria, and later, by his niece, another Caesaria. Caesarius wrote this Rule in successive periods, each one inspired by different authors. The first part depends on Pachomius, Cassian and the Fathers of Lerins; the second follows, step by step, the Rule of Saint Augustine. The third part, depending also on Lerins, gives regulations for the Divine Office, fasting and meals. It is followed by original legislation on the feminine problems of enclosure and clothing. In conclusion, there is a 'recapitulation' of the main precepts and warm exhortations to the sisters.

For these nuns also we have the letter, written to the second Caesaria by her cousin, the deacon (later priest and Abbot) Teridius, which is a kind of directory for the superior.

At the end of his life, Caesarius wrote the *Rule for Monks*, which is a summary of the one for nuns, expanded with scriptural quotations on the spiritual combat and fraternal charity. For them there are also his six sermons (233–238). In spite of the apparent disorder of these rules, some assertions stand out clearly from the text, by the frequency with which they occur.

The first, as we have seen, is poverty. The nuns must divest themselves of their goods, in writing, before entering the monastery. The habits must be simple and everything should be shared in common. Individual cupboards, private cells and keys are all forbidden.

In the same spirit of asceticism, fasting is also regulated, but the religious must have shown great fervour, for, in two places, it is found necessary to forbid fasting on Sundays. In contrast, the rather lengthy treatment given to anger and quarelling seems to indicate somewhat irascible temperaments. The enclosure, and separation from the world are also dealt with many times, as is normal for a monastery inside a town. As a whole, the precepts of the Rule favour an atmosphere of prayer in the monastery. The effort to advance towards God and unfailing attention to his word are recalled on every occasion.

The *Rule for Monks* indicates that the first three hours of the day are to be dedicated to *Lectio Divina*:

> In all seasons, one should be occupied in reading until Terce; then each goes to the work that is assigned to him.[8]

The *Rule for Nuns* comments:

> Meditation on the word of God and prayer from the heart should be continuous.[9]

In the same way, speaking of reading in the refectory, he says:

> Silence must be maintained at table and one must be attentive to the reading. When reading is finished, meditation in the heart must continue.[10]

A little further on, in a passage largely drawn from Augustine, a remark on fraternal charity becomes itself a prayer:

> That all may live in unity of spirit and in peace, honour God present in others, since you have deserved to become the Temple of God, according to the Gospel: 'Pray at all times, that you may be found worthy'. (*Luke 21: 36*); and the Apostle: 'Pray without ceasing'. (*1 Thess. 5:17*) When you pray to God in Psalms and hymns, let your heart repeat what your voice says. Whatever work you do, when there is no reading, 'ruminate' always on some passage of Scripture.

For the Office itself, Caesarius differentiates between Sundays and ordinary days, assigning to the latter two nocturns with three lessons at Matins, but six on Sundays, though the number of Psalms recited is not clearly indicated. His successor, Aurelian, who survived him by only a few years, laid down twelve Psalms for each nocturn, as many at Lauds and at each hour of the day. The hour of Compline only had no more than three Psalms.[11]

A last feature of the Rule of Caesarius is the care he takes to advise Abbot and Abbess. They are responsible for the well-being of the monastery. They must give to each member what is necessary, taking special care of the sick, and loving and correcting those under them. On their part, monks and nuns are urged to be obedient, to act with a pure heart and to cultivate harmony among themselves, so as to maintain in the house of God an atmosphere of peace and prayer. After an exhortation to self-sacrifice in humility, charity and patience, Caesarius ends with the portrait of the monk:

> He must be silent, gentle, humble and full of compunction, so that God and the angels may rejoice in our holy ways of living. (*nostra sancta conversatione*)[12]

Caesarius' *Rule for Nuns* has the distinction of being the first Rule written for women, and is the work of a bishop, writing to 'holy and venerable sisters' for whom he shows deep respect and true friendship. His exhortations at the end of the Rule demonstrate the importance he gives, in the life of the church, to their prayer of praise and intercession for the bishops and the people of God.

Notes

1 Sulpicius Severus, *Epist. III, 17 (ad Bassulam)* S.C. 133, p. 343; cf. Elie Griffe: *St Martin et le Monachisme gaulois*, in *St Martin et son Temps*, Studia Anselmiana 46, 1961.

2 The *Codex Regularum* of St Benedict of Aniane: P.L. 103.

3 The description of the Rules is based on A. de Vogüé, *Les Règles Monastiques Anciennes* (400–700) in *Typologie des Sources du Moyen Age Occidental*, ed. Brepols, 1985. cf. S.C. 297–298.

4 An abridged version of the *Rule of Pachomius*, however, was in circulation about the end of the fifth century in Italy.

5 We must also add the *Regula Communis*, depending on Fructuosus but chiefly on Jerome, and the *Regula Consensoria*, with some dependence

on the second Rule of the Fathers. Finally, in Gaul, another *regula cujusdam Patris* for men, deriving from Columbanus, Basil and Cassian.

6 Cassian, *Inst.* 2.

7 The Rules of Caesarius of Arles, S.C. 345 and 348.

8 Caesarius, *Rule for Monks*, c. 14, S.C. 348.

9 Caesarius, *Rule for Nuns*, c. 18, S.C. 345.

10 ibid. ch. 16.

11 Aurelian of Arles, *Rule for Monks*, P.L. 68, col. 393–395.

12 *Rule for Monks*, ch. 19.

CHAPTER XIV

The Rule of the Master
(*Regula Magistri*)

Author and plan of the Rule

Among Western rules, that of the Master plays a giant part. Three times as long as that of St Benedict, it also surpasses its forerunners by the richness of its contents, and, still more, by the methodical order with which it considers the different elements of monastic life. Finally, it has a particular importance for us, because it is the direct source of the Benedictine Rule and forms its principal link with Cassian.

The name of its author is unknown, but it seems that he lived near Rome, perhaps in the region of Subiaco, and that he drew up his Rule in the first quarter of the sixth century.[1]

The plan of the *Regula Magistri* is simple and well-organized. The introduction comprises a Prologue, which offers the Rule as the word of God and the key to the straight road that follows Christ. Then comes a 'thema', showing the monastery as the school of God's service for the sinful man, redeemed by baptism, who wishes to respond to the call of God. This development comprises two commentaries – first, one on the Pater, and then one on Psalms 33 and 14.[2]

This is followed by what the Master calls the Spiritual Art (*RM 3–6*). Chapter 1 describes different kinds of monks, dealing chiefly with cenobites in contrast to others. After that come directions for the Abbot, with an Appendix, which contains advice on how to counsel, and then, details of the *Spiritual Art* that he should practice (*chs 2–6*). Finally, chapters 7–10 are concerned with the three fundamental virtues: obedience, silence and humility.

The rest of the Rule is devoted to the organization of the monastery. This last and longest section begins by putting the programme of asceticism into practice with chapters on the Provost, excommunication, reconciliation and the open avowal of thoughts (*chs 11–15*). Then follows a section on meals and the officials who deal with them (*chs 16–28*), sleep (*chs 29–32*), the Office, its hours, composition and the manner of conducting it (*chs 33–49*), manual work, reading, and the norms proper to Lent (*chs 50–53*), and interferences with work, Office and journeys (*chs 54–68*). These first chapters on organization are followed by two complementary sections dealing with a variety of questions – care of the sick, the reception of guests, lateness (*chs 69–75*), clothing, the Abbot's table, the domains and produce of the monastery (*chs 80–86*) separated by chapters on guests (*chs 76–79*). A final section treats of the renewal of the monastery by means of the noviciate (*chs 87–91*) and the abbatial succession (*chs 92–94*). The rule ends with an appendix on the gate and gate-keepers (*ch. 95*).

Doctrine of the Rule of the Master

The originality of the Rule does not derive from elements added to previous monastic tradition, but in their integration in a single work, which for the first time in monastic history, attempts to comprise all the components of monastic life in a complete synthesis.

The teaching of the Master is based on an anthropology wherein man is composed of body, mind and spirit: the mind, the principle of freedom, faced with a choice between the attractions of the flesh and those of the spirit.[3] The structure of the community and monastic asceticism are then to form a central support with the idea of helping the monk to become 'spiritual', accomplishing the will of God by eliminating sin. Monastic life thus reveals itself as the 'narrow way' of the Gospel;[4] it is the prolongation of baptism, which makes us renounce evil to follow the call of the Lord, Master and Judge proclaimed in Scripture. Renouncing his own will, the monk, helped by the grace of

Christ, suffers with Him in order to share His glory.[5]

The monastery is to be a school of service to the Lord[6] where within the Church, a man applies himself to a 'special service of God'.[7] It will have its proper hierarchy, parallel to that of the Church, but within the Church and depending on her, for the Abbot is 'ordained' by the local bishop.[8] But in this school the Rule presents only the relationship between master and disciple, neglecting community aspects and the relations of monks with each other.[9] In this regard it is in line with the Desert Fathers, with the difference that the spiritual master does not derive his authority from some extraordinary charism, but from his consecration by the bishop. Another aspect is rather closer to the Pachomian tradition, namely, that the Abbot is bound, like the monks, to obey the Rule,[10] which is, in fact, regarded as an echo of Holy Scripture, transmitted by the Master, who, in his capacity of founder probably looked on himself as a 'teacher' and spokesman of God.[11]

> You, then, Listener, who hear me speak, listen not to what my mouth says, but to God, who speaks to you through this writing. (*R.M., Prologue*)

To lead the monk to avoid sin, the Rule makes full use of community pressure. The Abbot and the Provosts, by constant supervision, teach and control the monks so as to suppress the slightest failings.[12] Moreover, the Master naïvely introduced a kind of competition in virtue, the prize being no less than accession to the Abbatial seat.[13]

The personal effort required from the monk is described in the *Spiritual Art*, where, after a list of sins to be avoided and good works to be practised, three long treatises describe the ruling virtues, obedience, silence and humility.[14] Here also they are considered in the light of the struggle against sin. Obedience cuts short self-will and carnal desires. It must be total, confiding blindly in the superior, who alone bears the responsibility for what is done. Safeguarding of the heart, modesty of gaze, and silence, arrest sin at human nature's most vulnerable points. Humility includes the other virtues and perfects them by achieving the specific remedy against pride. The Rule aims also at guiding the monk in his ascent towards God. But, in spite of an attempt at classification in the degrees of humility, the Master scarcely makes any theoretic speculation and his counsels follow each other without much order. It is worthy of note, however, that, like Cassian, he requires absolute renunciation of material possessions,[15] and mastery over vice and outward conduct,[16] so as to lead the brother to become perfect or 'spiritual'. For the more advanced monks, the Master has a special and more exacting rule,[17] aimed at leading them to perfect charity and to the grace of the Spirit that purifies the heart from all vice and sin.[18] This care for the spiritual also dictates the choice of work to be undertaken, and he invites the monks so to arrange matters as to avoid worldly cares, and devote themselves entirely to the search for God.[19]

We recognize in general a number of ideas derived from Cassian, but there are two points on which the borrowings are more specific. The Master avails himself of the signs of humility described in the *Institutes*[20] to write his chapter on the same subject, but is especially indebted to him for his arrangement of the Office, where he allots six to twelve Psalms for the night hours and three for the day,[21] a contrast in its brevity with the practice in Gallic monasteries.

The qualities of organization in the Rule of the Master are unfortunately obscured by faults which have hindered its diffusion. Even if one ignores the digressions and the inelegancies that rebuff the modern reader, but were perhaps less offensive in his own time, the fact remains that the Master is swamped in the minutiae of casuistry and ceremonial detail, so that his Rule is inapplicable outside the milieu for which it was written.

As a conclusion to this chapter we may notice how the Western Rules draw on the same Biblical texts that had inspired their predecessors in the East, and interpret them in the same way. Within a less varied framework, they adopt the great directives of their cenobitic life. Humility, obedience, charity and patience are the primary virtues of the monk. Fasts, vigils, poverty, manual labour and silence provide a support; all is orientated towards prayer, nour-ished by the Office, by sacred reading and 'rumination' over texts of Scripture. This prayer must be frequent, even, continual, for the presence of God dwells in us. Within this undisputed framework, each legislator might inscribe the detailed regulations that circumstances or his own tempera-ment would suggest to him.

Such was the heritage that St Benedict received from his Western brethren. He, no doubt, had no other ambition than to outline a rule for his own monks, following the custom of his time. But in doing so, his genius and the inspi-ration of the Holy Spirit led him to work out, from concrete situations, the principles of monastic life gathered from the experience of the Fathers and still valid for us.

Notes

1 For the *Rule of the Master*, which we indicate by the sign R.M., we have followed the edition made by Adalbert de Vogüé in *Sources Chrétiennes* in three volumes (105, 106, 107).
2 We have used, as in the work above, the sign Thp for the commentary of the Father and Ths for that of the Psalms.
3 This division which has its origin in St Paul, was developed by Origen and transmitted to the Master by Cassian. In RM, Thp 28; 1, 80; 81, 18–19.
4 This is the whole object of the Prologue.
5 These themes are developed in the two parts of the Thema.
6 Ths 45.
7 RM 28.
8 RM 93.
9 A. de Vogüé, loc. cit. t. 1 pp. 117–118.
10 Its observation is the criterion for the choice of the Abbot (RM 92); it is central in the ceremony of ordination (RM 93). See A. de Vogüé, loc. cit. p. 120.
11 Prologue, 2.
12 RM 17, 8; 19, 13; 73, 3–4, 7.
13 RM the whole of 92, particularly 48–49.
14 RM Obedience: ch. 7; Silence: ch. 8–9: Humility: ch. 10.
15 RM ch. 87 to 91.
16 RM ch. 7 to 10, ch. 90 throughout.
17 The chapters on obedience and silence have this special feature; fervent monks are often called 'spiritual', RM 27, 47–51; 44, 17–18; 55, 13).
18 RM 10, 91.

19 RM ch. 82, 85, 86, 91, and throughout.
20 Cassian *Inst.* IV, 39, 2.
21 RM ch. 33–37. The Master favoured a longer Office of Matins in Winter. St Benedict returned to the norm given by Cassian, of twelve Psalms for all seasons.

CHAPTER XV

St Benedict

His life (480–547)

All we know about St Benedict comes from Pope St Gregory the Great who made the 2nd book of his *Dialogues* into an account of his life, written about the year 593. He based this account on the testimonies given by monks who had known him. This search for authentic history gives us a guarantee that at least the essential traits of his life and character are exact.

Benedict was born about the year 480 at Nursia, a little town about 70 miles north-east of Rome. As a young man, he was sent to Rome to do his studies. Some passages in his Rule suggest that he may have read law. However, he soon became disgusted by the behaviour of his fellow-students and left the city, taking refuge first among the fervent Christians of Affile, and then in a cave at Subiaco. There he received the monastic habit from a monk called Romanus, who also brought him food. Benedict lived there 'dwelling alone with himself, in the presence of his heavenly Father ... keeping watch over himself, he remained in the presence of his Creator'.[1]

For all that, he was not exempt from temptations: one day, driven to distraction by the memory of a woman, he had to roll in the nettles so that the pain of their stings might drive away the fire of passion.

After three years he was discovered in his cave; so he began to catechize the local shepherds, and disciples came to him. The monks of a nearby monastery asked him to succeed their recently deceased abbot, but were unable to cope with Benedict's discipline. When he discovered that they had attempted to poison him, he returned quietly to his solitude and occupied himself with teaching his disciples. For these he set up twelve little monasteries, whose memory still remains in the area around the cave. Only one survived and developed, now called 'Saint Scholastica's', near to the town of Subiaco.

Benedict's success caused a certain priest to become jealous and try to make the young brothers of the monastery leave by bringing a troupe of women to dance in front of the garden. But Benedict, aware that this was against his own person, decided to leave Subiaco and establish himself at Monte Cassino where he built a bigger monastery, wrote his Rule, and took care of the poor in time of famine and war.

It was there, also, that his sister, Scholastica, 'consecrated to God since her adolescence' came to visit once a year and she is considered as the spiritual ancestor of Benedictine women. Three days after her last visit, the holy woman died and Benedict had her buried in the tomb he had prepared for himself. A few years later, knowing that his hour had come, he had himself carried to the chapel and, his arms raised in prayer, he gave his soul back to God. According to tradition it was 21st March 547, but it may have been a few years later.

BENEDICT: Meeting-point between East and West

St Benedict's life-time – the end of the fifth and first half of the sixth century – witnessed the encounter in Rome of the Eastern and Western monastic traditions. St Antony's life was already well known and, at that time, Latin translations of St Basil's *Asceticon*, of Pachomius' *Rules* and of the Desert Fathers' *Sayings* were made. In the same period appeared the works of Cassian, the Life of St Martin and several monastic Rules written in Gaul and in Italy (Lerins, Arles, *Rule of the Master*). St Benedict was thus placed in a unique point in history, at the meeting-place of the Eastern tradition with the first Western Rules, and he had the genius to make a synthesis of the main spiritual values handed down to him.

The Rule of St Benedict

The plan of St Benedict's Rule, mostly borrowed from that of the Master, is simple, despite a certain lack of order due to some suppressions and additions.

The first part deals with spiritual matters: the aim of the Rule, the spirit of the monastery, the abbot's role with his council, the list of 'good works' and the chapters on the main monastic virtues: obedience, silence, humility. The second part is more institutional; it gives the organization of prayer, the means of correction to foster repentance, the rules for material life: meals, clothing, time-table. Then come relations with the outside world: journeys, guests, gifts and finally the renewal of the community by receiving novices and appointing the abbot. Added at the end are a few but important chapters on the fraternal relations and the higher degrees of the spiritual life.

THE SPIRITUALITY OF ST BENEDICT

Truly seeking God

The essential quality that Benedict wants to find in those who knock on the door of the monastery is that they be 'truly seeking God', with a zeal for prayer and for humility.[2] To consecrate one's life to search above all for union with God or the Absolute is the common point which unites monks, no matter which religion they belong to. This common goal explains the similarity between the means used to attain it. Benedict defines them in his Rule.

The obedience of the heart to the 'divine precepts'

Listen, my son, to your Master's precepts, and incline the ear of your heart. Receive willingly, and carry out effectively your loving father's advice, that by the labour of obedience, you may return to Him from whom you had departed by the sloth of disobedience ... you are renouncing your own will to do battle under the Lord Christ, the true King, and taking up the strong, bright weapons of obedience.[3]

These first lines of the Rule show that, for St Benedict, obedience is not just doing what is asked by the Superior, but a disposition of the heart to follow Christ in his conformity to the desires of the Father.

The monk to whom St Benedict speaks is a 'cenobite', that is, someone who 'lives in a monastery and serves under a Rule and an Abbot'.[4] God's intentions will be thus made manifest first by the community, for Christ is present in each of his members. Hence the care for the weak, mutual respect, and obedience and the role of the councils of the elders and of the community. The Abbot consults them when 'any important business has to be done' and 'the Lord often reveals to the younger what is best'.[5]

The aim of the Rule is to show the monk how to put in practice these dispositions of heart in the various situations of his life. The abbot also represents Christ in his duty of giving the community a unity and spiritual dynamism by his words and example. When a difficult decision is to be taken, it must be preceded by a frank dialogue with the one concerned, who then 'obeys out of love, trusting in the help of God'.[6]

Silence: mastery of words and thoughts

God makes himself heard in interior silence. In order to attain this silence one must avoid chatter and evil conversation.[7] But, at the same time, one must cultivate the 'good word': the kind of speech which helps, guides and comforts.[8] The same positive action is used in the realm of the intellect: bad or useless thoughts disappear of themselves when they are replaced by the word of Scripture, meditated in the heart.

Humility

Using the ladder of humility whose outlines had been drawn by Cassian and the Rule of the Master, Benedict presents, in chapter 7 of his Rule, the twelve degrees of humility as a programme of the spiritual life: the reminder of the constant presence of God helps one to move away from selfish desires, and follow the Lord, fulfilling the will of his Father (1–2). The monk holds on to obedience and patience in his trials (3–4) and is helped by revealing his thoughts to the spiritual father (5), by simplicity, which enables him to remain in his place and conform to the local customs (6–8), and finally, by silence, well-chosen words and an attitude of mutual respect (9–12). At the top of the ladder is the perfect love of God, a gift of the Spirit which purifies the heart and makes the following of Christ a joyful and quasi-natural thing.

Scripture and the liturgy
The very natural way in which Benedict quotes Scripture shows that his thought was completely penetrated by it. To arrive at that result he recommends that the monks 'stand to sing the psalms in such a way that their minds may be in harmony with their voices'.[9]

The recitation of the Office follows the cycle of the liturgical year, but this set the tone for the whole life of the monastery, which is centred on the feast of Easter. Each period has its corresponding time-table and a dietary regime with fasting days. The body sustains the spirit in following the unfolding of the mysteries of Christ and in living them out throughout the year.

Equilibrium: prayer, lectio, work
The monk's day is divided into three almost equal parts which complement and balance one another:

Prayer
The recitation of the Divine Office begins at night and makes use of the natural intervals between periods of work during the day.[10] In addition, St Benedict says 'whatever good work you begin, beg of Christ with most earnest prayer to perfect it'.[11] The monk can thus offer all that he does to God.[12] Personal prayer is recommended as a normal way of prolonging the office and lectio.

Lectio Divina
It is the study and meditative reading of Scripture and other texts which nourish faith. The monk enters into the sense of the text and applies it to his personal life in order to moti-

vate himself or rectify his daily activity. The words which touch the heart and put him in contact with God are retained in the memory and repeated interiorly so that he remains in his presence during the day and lives his mysteries more deeply.

Work

'Then are they truly monks, when they live by the work of their hands, as did our Fathers and the Apostles'.[13] St Benedict wants his disciples to work in order to make their living and help the poor. His life shows that he often shared in the work of the community. But, beyond this social dimension, manual labour contributes towards a human equilibrium by giving the ability to control one's own body, which is a very useful thing for meditation.

Hospitality

'All guests that come to the monastery should be received like Christ'.[14] The guests are received in an atmosphere of peace and prayer, 'giving to each one the honour which is his due'[15] with a special attention for the poor and for the servants of God. St Benedict himself received kings as well as peasants and gave his last bottle of oil to a subdeacon, in time of famine. Ever since then, monasteries have always been open to those who come to them seeking peace.

Koinonia: fraternal communion

The traditional term *Koinonia* indicates the charity which unites the members of the community. St Benedict often returns to this point and ends his Rule with two chapters (71–72), on mutual obedience and respect, a 'good zeal practised with the most fervent love' which leads to God and unites the community. 'The brethren are to obey one another ... anticipate one another in honour, endure most patiently one another's infirmities, whether of body or of character, vie in paying obedience one to another. No-one should follow what he considers useful for himself but rather what benefits another'.[16] In another place he writes 'One should respect the seniors and love the juniors'.[17]

When he is correcting the brothers, the abbot 'should

hate vices but love the brethren ... remembering that the bruised reed must not be broken ... Let him study rather to be loved than to be feared'.[18] At the end of the Rule, St Benedict unites in the same love brethren, abbot and Christ 'that he may bring us all together to everlasting life'.[19]

Discretion and adaptability

St Gregory the Great ends his life of St Benedict by praising his Rule for its 'discretion'. Indeed, Chapter 64 of the Rule requires the abbot to be 'prudent and considerate ... discreet and moderate', practising 'discretion, the mother of virtues, let him temper all things that the strong may have something to strive after and the weak may not fall back in dismay'.[20]

This discretion is seen also in the duty the abbot has of adapting the Rule to the circumstances of the time and place. In his Rule, Benedict shows the interior attitude of the monk rather than prescribing the minutiae. He leaves it to the abbot to adapt the principles which he puts forward in a manner suitable for his time and place. This fluidity and balance ensured that the Rule of St Benedict would spread, first throughout the West and, later, throughout the entire world, spanning the centuries and adapting itself to every culture.

Notes

 1 St. Gregory *Dialogues* S.C. 251, 260, 265.
 2 RB 58, 7.
 3 RB Prol 1–3
 4 RB 1:2
 5 RB 3:1, 3
 6 RB 68:2–5
 7 RB 6:1–5; 7:56–58.
 8 RB 4:18–19; 7:60–61; 27:3–4; 31:13
 9 RB 19, 7
10 RB 8–19
11 RB Prol 4
12 RB 20
13 RB 48:9
14 RB 53:1
15 RB 53:2

16 RB 72:2–7
17 RB 4:68–69
18 RB 64:11,15
19 RB 73:12
20 RB 64:17–19

CHAPTER XVI

St Bernard

In his Rule, St Benedict had condensed the experience of his predecessors concerning the monastic life as a way leading to God. Several expressions in this Rule – and also what Pope St Gregory the Great says about his life – make one feel that he must have had a profound mystical experience. But, in order to describe it, he contents himself by suggesting that his readers refer to Cassian and the Fathers of the Church. His disciple, St Bernard, makes up for this lack by describing the stages on the way to God, basing himself on the Rule. He adds his own touches by developing the theme of the love of Christ, already emphasized by St Benedict, and the role which Mary plays in the sanctification of the Church.

His life[1] (1090–1153)

Born in France, near Dijon, in 1090, Bernard entered the monastery of Cîteaux in 1112, at the end of his classical studies, bringing with him thirty of his relatives and friends. His abbot, St Stephen Harding, sent him, in 1115, to found the monastery of Clairvaux, where he would be abbot until his death in 1153. During his long abbacy he founded 68 monasteries which themselves founded a hundred others spread throughout the whole of Europe, from Sweden to Portugal and in Sicily.

Like every abbot, Bernard taught his monks and commented on the Rule for them. In the degrees of humility, described in chapter VII, he found a ladder of charity, showing how it could increase or diminish in the heart of the monk. In 1119, he published his teachings to the monks in his treatise on 'The Degrees of Humility and of Pride' (*De gradibus humilitatis et superbiae*). After 1122, he became a spiritual master whose authority and influence was felt throughout Christendom. From that time onwards he was always travelling, responding to the requests he received from princes, bishops and Popes to help resolve conflicts and to rejuvenate the fervour of the religious life of the Church and of monastic communities. Despite this intense activity, St Bernard remained above all a contemplative and the principal themes of his works concern the spiritual life.

ST BERNARD, MASTER OF THE SPIRITUAL LIFE

His personality

Right from his adolescence, Bernard liked to 'dwell with himself and reflect'. Later, at Clairvaux, his spirit was so completely absorbed in meditation that he would 'look without seeing and hear without hearing'.[2] He would meditate above all on Holy Scripture and was so saturated by it that the language of the holy books became the expression of his own thought.[3] In addition, he would read the Fathers, especially St Augustine, St Gregory the Great, St Ambrose, Cassian and Origen and St Gregory of Nyssa.[4]

In his monastic observance Bernard cultivated the spirit of Cîteaux: that is a desire to return to the sources and an observance, as literal as possible, of the Rule of St Benedict in a life divided between the Divine Office, manual labour and *Lectio Divina* (a meditative reading of the Scriptures and the Fathers). It is also the virtue of 'simplicity', which helps to remove all that is superfluous.

This taste for 'interiorization' and simplicity marks all the spirituality of our saint. Not finding God except within himself, he had a horror of all which led to dissipation, hence his condemnation of the Cluniac monks' sculptural imagery.

His teaching on the love of God

One could say that, in all his works, Bernard speaks only of love: the love of God for the human race and the diverse forms of the human response to that love: humanity searches for the One who searches for it. 'Love gives love' (*caritas dat caritatem*).[5]

We have already seen that Bernard discovered a ladder of love in the seventh chapter of the Rule of St Benedict, something which would influence all his works. When he was ill in 1122, he meditated on the Song of Songs, a book on which he wrote eighty-six sermons during the course of his life, without ever completing it. In 1126 he wrote a treatise 'On the love of God' (*De diligendo Deo*) and, later, did the same for 'Grace and Free Will' (*De gratia et libero arbitrio*) in which he discussed the nature of the human soul and its response to the love of God. In his letters, treatises and sermons St Bernard always returns to union with God by means of love.[6] The point of departure is conversion from 'carnal love', or selfish love, to the love of one's neighbour and to the love of God.

Conversion from 'carnal love'

Love of self is good, according to human nature but it is perverted by the selfish desire for empty things (*curiositas*). This leads to ignorance, which makes one choose things which only appear to be good. Conversion begins with a return to oneself by means of humility, that is, a real awareness of one's condition, so that one can take one's place before God. The image of the Prodigal Son is often used by St Bernard to describe this change. Following the ladder of St Benedict, humility leads from self-love to a love of one's neighbour and to the various stages of the love of God.

'Mercenary' love of God

This is a true love which contains a faithful obedience in which the soul also looks for its own advantage; an anxious love purified by trials and perfected by the contemplation of God's attributes and of the mysteries of Christ's life.

Filial love

This assists 'mercenary' love by giving it a devotion which enables it to become disinterested and progressively purifies it from its selfishness, putting back into order the desires of the body and the soul. It is developed by the consideration of God's goodness. Thus love becomes more and more true and prepares for union with God.

Mystical love

Like St Benedict, St Bernard, in all his works, places perfect charity at the summit of the ladder of humility; he considers it to be a gift of God and a participation in the life of the Holy Trinity, which is love itself. This love gradually transforms the soul, destroying its selfishness and producing a perfect accord between the human will and that of God. Thus the soul adheres to God and becomes one spirit with him.[7] The effect of this union in the soul is an *excessus* or a 'going beyond' its natural capacities. This gift sets it free from all desire or fear, illuminating its interior senses, allowing it to penetrate the meaning of the Scriptures and the divine mysteries.

Spousal love

Finally the soul, thus elevated, becomes the spouse of the Word, entering into the peace of the 'nuptial chamber' where 'the tranquillity of God tranquillizes everything' (*Tranquillus Deus tranquillat universa*).[8] It is the conformity of the will with that of the Word which unites it to him:

> the soul shows itself to be as loving as it is loved. Thus the one who loves perfectly becomes the spouse.[9]

The soul co-operates with the divine action by its burning desire for the Word like the Bride in the Song of Songs.[10]

However, Bernard does not spend much time in describing the heights of mystical experience – 'rare and unforeseen' moments – but he recognizes in himself the transforming presence of the Word:

it was by the movement of my heart that I recognized that He was there. I acknowledged his strength and his power in the quietening of my vices and my passions ... I experienced his sweetness and goodness in the slight improvement of my life.[11]

Bernard's spirituality emphasizes ethics, the virtues necessary for union with God and the strength of the grace which draws one towards Him. In this, the Abbot of Clairvaux follows St Benedict, who always unites the listening of the heart with virtuous action:

incline the ear of your heart ... receive **willingly** and carry out **effectively** your loving Father's advice.[12]

To these various ways of union with God, which have their counterpart in the writings of his predecessors, Bernard added his own personal stamp, which had a great influence on the monastic life and the mysticism in the following centuries.

SPECIAL CHARACTERISTICS OF THE SPIRITUALITY OF ST BERNARD

Meditation on the mystery of Christ's humanity

The central point of St Bernard's teaching is that, if one wants to go to God, one needs to become like Christ, 'to follow his way'. His prayer focused on the Word as Man, Jesus. To reach the love of the Word which is spirit, he saw that it is necessary to start with the love of the Word made flesh. Meditating on the mysteries of the life of Jesus, he followed the cycle of the liturgical year, like St Benedict. The interior contact with the words of Scripture, especially as they are lived in the liturgy, has a transforming power over the soul: 'they work in each person like a healing medicine'.[13]

The sufferings, the humility and the compassion of Christ produce charity and obedience to God in the soul.

The principal reason for which the invisible God wanted to come in the flesh, was that he could first draw all human affections to the salutary love of his flesh ... and to lead them on, step by step, to spiritual love.[14]

Thus the 'carnal' and 'felt' love for Christ must be surpassed, or rather, enriched by the spiritual love for the Word, Wisdom and Holiness.

This love means to become like Christ, and since the Word is the image of the Father 'we need his example and help so that we can become like him'[15]. This loving 'concord' is mutual agreement between the human will and the divine will. It is a shared work of grace and freedom.

We find here once more the spousal love in which the soul searches for the Word, and aspires to union with him, contemplating him and rejoicing in his peace, like the bride in the Canticle. The Word makes her fertile by inspiring an apostolic zeal within her.

Bernard 'Minstrel of Mary'

If the Word is the image of the Father, Mary, by means of her divine motherhood, is the creature who is closest to Christ. She is the 'new Eve', associated with the 'new Adam' and she works with her Son for the sanctification of the Church. For humans, she is 'a model of their own kind'.[16] Mary is an instrument through which Christ can send out his grace: like him, she has come 'not to be served, but to serve', she is like an aquaduct which is adapted to our weakness and brings us the grace of Christ, increasing purity and humility within us so that we can come to the perfection of charity. By her example and her intercession 'the Virgin queen is herself the channel through which her Son comes'.[17]

Mary, however, is not isolated. With her, the angels and the saints strengthen us with their example and their intercession. Together, they form the invisible part of the Church, which protects us from the forces of evil.

AFTER BERNARD

The return to the Rule of St Benedict and the reforming zeal of St Bernard have had an enduring influence on the monastic world, inspiring successive renewals in the course of the centuries, among Benedictines just as much as among Cistercians.

In western spirituality his influence has also been great in the way that he emphasized devotion to the persons of Christ and Mary, his Mother. Traces of this can be seen in St Bonaventure and the Franciscan school, in the *devotio moderna* and the *Imitation of Christ* as well as in the later French school with Bérulle.

Let us note only his immediate followers who still influence monastic spirituality: his disciples, William of St Thierry, with his *Commentary on the Song of Songs* and Aelred of Rievaulx, with his *Mirror of Charity*. Later, Guigo II the Carthusian in his *Scala Paradisi* or 'Ladder for Cloister-Dwellers' (monks) systematized the way of monastic contemplation coming from *Lectio Divina* by defining its stages as reading, meditation, prayer, contemplation.

The nuns of Helfta, St Gertrude and St Mechtilde, composed meditations based on the texts of the liturgy with a Christocentric emphasis, using images drawn from the Bible and everyday life. Their devotion to Mary as 'Mother of our Souls' is always dependent on Christ.[18]

Though St Bernard is sometimes called 'the last of the Fathers' he does not end the list of those who have contributed to Christian spirituality. He brought to light new fields of contemplation and later schools would unveil other aspects which continue to enrich the Church. These varieties of spirituality allow the diverse vocations and temperaments to progress towards God in the security and joy of being His children.

Notes

1 cf. D. Anselme LE Bail. *Dict. de Spiritualité*, Art S. Bernard; D. Charles Dumont S. Bernard Mystique selon la Règle de S. Benoit, *Lettre de Ligugé* 206, 1981; La Spiritualité de S. Bernard *Nouvelle Revue Théologique*, 112, 1990; L'action contemplative, le temps

dans l'éternité d'après S. Bernard *Collectanea Cist.* 4, 1992.

2 St Bernard, *Vita Prima*, 228; 238. The expression 'to dwell with himself' is an allusion to the passage in the life of St Benedict by St Gregory the Great where the spirit of recollection of the Father of monks is described.

3 ibid. 241.

4 St Bernard's language is simple – it is the Latin of the *Vulgate* (the translation of the Bible existing at that time) – and his treatment follows the methods of the early scholastics, enriched with a heartfelt warmth which gives it all its charm.

5 *De Diligendo Deo* C.12; cf. *In Cant. Cant.* 84:5

6 The works of St Bernard are usually divided into sermons, letters and treatises which included Rules for various religious orders in formation, e.g. The Templars and, unique of its kind, the *De Consideratione*, advice given to one of his monks who became Pope Eugene III. We do not have space here to give a complete list but the most important works will be mentioned as occasion arises.

7 cf. *De Diligendo Deo* c.11; Sermon 11 *In Cant. Cant.*

8 *In Cant. Cant.* PL 183, col. 893.

9 *In Cant. Cant.* PL 183, col. 1182.

10 *In Cant. Cant.* Serm. 52 and 83.

11 *In Cant. Cant.* 74:6.

12 RB Prol. 1.

13 *De gratia et libero arbitrio*, PL 182, col. 1019.

14 *In Cant. Cant.* 6.

15 *De gratia et libero arbitrio*, PL 182, col. 1019.

16 *De duodecim praerogative B.M.V. Mariae*, PL 183, col 1.434ss.

17 *De acquaeductu*, PL 183, col. 437–448; *In Adventu*, Sermo. 2. n. 4–5.

18 cf. the *Spiritual Exercises* of St Gertrude, her *Revelations* and the *Revelations* of St Mechtilde, probably transcribed by Gertrude herself.

Non-Christian Doctrines and Heresies that have Influenced Early Christian Monachism

MANICHEISM

This religion was founded by a man called Mani. He belonged to a noble family of Babylon where he was born about A.D. 216. His teaching spread throughout the Middle East, Europe and Asia. Persecution drove it from Europe in the sixth century, from the East in the ninth and from Central Asia in the thirteenth.

In the moral sphere, Manicheans thought they had the redemptive mission of co-operating together to separate light from darkness. Their manner of eating was meant to set free the light mingled with matter in plants, whence a triple abstinence – that of the lips, which abstained from meat, wine and from uttering insults; that of the hands, forbidding manual work, ownership, war, agriculture, the act of killing and the use of fire; that of the inner organs, abstaining from procreation and sexual relationships. Some pushed their contempt for matter and the body to the point of committing suicide. These prohibitions were safeguarded by vows, taken by the perfect or the 'Chosen', whose souls, after death, passed directly into the kingdom of light. The other members, or 'hearers', were bound by a much laxer observance, but had to be reincarnated as 'chosen ones' in order to be saved.

Manicheism exercised a strong influence in Syria and in Egypt, where at times it was indistinguishable from

Marcionism (heresy of the second century). Certain Christian ascetics adopted its customs, fasting on bread and water, abstaining from cooked food, scorning the body and refraining from washing themselves.

Christian spiritual writers reacted against these tendencies. The Desert Fathers insisted on the duty of working, both to earn one's living and to give alms, and on moderation and avoidance of all excess. They also recommended meditation on the whole canon of Scripture. St Basil and the Cappadocian Fathers, while praising virginity, taught that it must be observed for God's sake and not out of scorn for marriage.

THE MESSALIANS

The Messalians also followed a current of dualistic thought, non-Christian in origin. They believed that good and evil were two realities (sometimes two spiritual beings), either actually living in the soul or taking possession of its faculties. They also said that baptism was useless, since it did not suppress the presence of evil in the soul, nor its power of attraction over it. Work, marriage, almsgiving were evil, for all material things belonged to the domain of darkness. The body itself was evil; it must be despised and neglected. Prayer alone was good; it was the source of illumination, and each must follow the lights thus received.

The Messalians spread through almost the whole of the Middle East, especially in Syria, Cappadocia and Palestine. Their influence on Christianity manifested itself chiefly by an exaggerated asceticism, which was put into practice by Eustathius of Sebaste and his disciples.

The Christian reaction to these tendencies is most clearly expressed by St Basil and the Cappadocian Fathers, who insisted that monks earn their living by work and guide their lives, not by private revelations, but in accordance with the Gospel, seeking the will of God in obedience, and disregarding their own will. Instead of extraordinary penances, the Fathers taught moderation. Lastly, in opposition to the theory that the soul was the dwelling place of the devil, they insisted on the existence in man of free-will.

The errors of the Messalians also were responsible for new developments in Christian monastic thought. Suspicion of false mysticism drove the Fathers, particularly Gregory of Nyssa, to give a more precise description of Christian mysticism and its effects on the soul. Finally, in reply to the claim that baptism was ineffectual, they pointed to monastic life as a proof of the action of the Holy Spirit in the soul, and this led them to regard religious profession and compunction of heart as a second baptism.

ORIGENISM

The doctrines assigned to this name are not the complete teachings of Origen, but a current of thought that arose from certain speculations set forth in the *De principiis* and later systematized between the fourth and the sixth century.

The principal errors are: first a certain subordination within the Trinity. Not distinguishing clearly between the order of origin and that of dignity, they imagined a kind of hierarchy in God. The Son and the Holy Spirit were considered also as intermediaries between creatures and the Father.

Next, in considering creation, Origen works on two planes as did the Gnostic system. The higher world admits of God the Father, transcendent and incomprehensible. He eternally engenders the Son in His image, at once one and many, incomprehensible and comprehensible. In the third place come spiritual creatures, pure spirits, initially all equal and sharing in the Logos. In a second period, all these spirits fell through their fault in letting their love grow lukewarm. As a consequence God united them with bodies, more or less heavy and they organized themselves in a universe which embraces demons in the lowest place, angels in the highest, and men in the middle. Human existence, therefore, is given to these spirits as a fresh opportunity for struggle and victory. The different degrees of grace and the differences between men are explained by the greater and lesser gravity of the faults committed in a previous world.

Lastly, in a third period, the Word of God, by a salutary dispensation, reclaims all these wills in order to convert them to God. The bodies will be glorified and then disappear in a union with the Divine. Men, and even demons, will thus be saved 'by the purification of fire', and restored to their primal state of pure spirit. For this a succession of worlds is necessary. This perspective denies the true historicity of the Messiah, which is the distinctive feature of Christianity, and dilutes the action of Christ in a cosmic process.[1]

Among the chief Origenists, Evagrius Ponticus must be mentioned first. In his *Letter to Melania and his Gnostic Chapters*, he assembled these theories into a rational system, which was to provoke their condemnation by Bishop Theophilus of Alexandria, and the persecution against Origenist monks. A little later (from the fifth to the sixth century), in Syria and Palestine, the 'Isochrists' took up the system again in a pantheistic form.

The condemnation of Origen – as seen through Evagrius – was promulgated by Justinian in the *Letter to Menas* in 543, and the Second Council of Constantinople condemned the Isochrists in 554.

Notes

1   See Daniélou, *The First Six Hundred Years* pp. 185, 186. It must be noted also that, in the interpretation of Scripture, Origen is mistaken in maintaining that 'Everything has a spiritual meaning, but not everything has a literal meaning'. The contrary is true. Moreover, this allegorical interpretation leads him to be sometimes subjective and arbitrary.